GHOST WRITERS

THE HALLOWED HAUNTS
OF UNFORGETTABLE
LITERARY ICONS

SAM BALTRUSIS

Globe
Pequot

Guilford, Connecticut

Globe
Pequot

An imprint of The Rowman & Littlefield Publishing Group, Inc.
4501 Forbes Blvd., Ste. 200
Lanham, MD 20706
www.rowman.com

Distributed by NATIONAL BOOK NETWORK

British Library Cataloguing in Publication Information available

Library of Congress Cataloging-in-Publication Data available

ISBN 978-1-4930-4368-2 (paperback)
ISBN 978-1-4930-4369-9 (e-book)

♾™ The paper used in this publication meets the minimum requirements of American National Standard for Information Sciences—Permanence of Paper for Printed Library Materials, ANSI/ NISO Z39.48-1992

CONTENTS

FOREWORD

"We put ourselves in the middle of some disturbingly dangerous battles so we can document and share our experiences with others."
—JONI MAYHAN, AUTHOR AND PARANORMAL INVESTIGATOR

The first time I heard author Sam Baltrusis talk about his book *Ghost Writers* was at a vendor table I was sharing with him at a paranormal convention in Salem, Massachusetts.

A paracon isn't your typical, run-of-the-mill event. They attract enthusiasts from all walks of life. Some of them are spectators, while others sell their wares or promote their teams. There are psychic mediums offering readings, investigation teams promoting their groups, and vendors who sell a variety of products. A few paranormal-themed authors also attend, hoping to bring awareness to their books.

Because Sam and I have been friends for years, it made sense for us to share a table.

Many people didn't understand this. "Aren't you competitors?" they'd ask, wondering why we'd share space with the enemy. The truth is, we might be competitors, but we're also collaborators. We learned early on that readers read more than one book. If they've read my books, hopefully they'll also read Sam's books and vice versa. Since that first paracon, we've helped one another. We've aided each other with editing, have shared stories in each other's books, and have opened the pipeline for other authors to join our alliance.

It just makes sense. Together we're stronger than we are separately. No man or woman is an island in the paranormal field, which was why we found it so odd that paranormal authors weren't invited to be speakers at the paracons.

Most of the paranormal conventions offered a stage in another room where visitors could listen to an assortment of experts in the field talk about their encounters. As we looked at the lineup, we were astounded to notice that every single speaker was a television personality. While we both understood the need to use celebrities to increase attendance, we wondered why weren't they interspersing with others—authors, investigators, and researchers—in the field? The usual suspects from television weren't the only ones who knew a thing or two about the other side. Besides ourselves, we knew dozens of people who were enormously knowledgeable about the paranormal world. Why not invite them to speak as well?

After this conversation, Sam took the wheel and set up his own paracon, one that would offer a diverse mixture of both worlds. Due to scheduling conflicts, I wasn't able to attend his first conference, held in Provincetown, Massachusetts, but I did fly back to attend his Plymouth ParaCon in 2018 with para-celebs such as John Zaffis from the *Haunted Collector* and Doogie and Porter from *Haunted Towns*. At the event I was offered my first opportunity to be a speaker at a ghost-themed convention. I invited my friend Gare Allen, who is also a paranormal author and collaborator, to share the stage with me. We spent an hour talking about the haunted towns we've both written about. While I spoke about *Haunted New Harmony*, Gare talked about *Haunted Tampa*. The room was packed with listeners, many of whom stayed to ask us questions. We also met other authors, such as Darcy H. Lee who wrote *Ghosts of Plymouth, Massachusetts*, and Jack Kenna, who wrote *Paranormal Research: A Comprehensive Guide to Building a Strong Team*. They were both invited to speak at the annual event.

The Plymouth ParaCon was a major success and we all left feeling as though we'd accomplished something monumental. Sam had broken the mold and created something of which we were all proud to be a part because of its diversity of speakers.

During our years of friendship, Sam and I have also found ourselves talking about our experiences in the paranormal world. It's impossible to write about the supernatural without experiencing it firsthand and we've both lived through our fair share of horrific events. Once we realized we were in the same metaphysical boat, both with our writing and our paranormal encounters, we began helping each other even more.

"Weren't you nervous about publishing your first paranormal book?" Sam asked. He didn't have to explain his question any further. I knew exactly what he meant. Putting yourself out there to the world as someone who's experienced something bizarre and sometimes unbelievable is a brave conquest. You open yourself up to scrutiny and backlash. The flip-side to this is that you also help people.

When I considered publishing my first paranormal book, *Soul Collector*, in 2013, I was terrified. Not only was I strongly warned by my mentors to not discuss my experience for fear I'd draw the nasty entity back to me, I was also worried about how people might react. What would my family in Indiana think when they read it? What about my former coworkers and acquaintances who had no idea about my other life? And what about the nameless readers who would pick up my book without knowing me? Some of the things that happened to me were so strange and otherworldly that I feared people might think I was making it all up for the sake of a profit.

After much soul searching, I finally took a leap of faith and published my book. While I was expecting backlash and harassment, reactions were far different.

Hundreds of people reached out to me, having lived through similar horrors. They applauded my courage to "come out" about my medium-ship abilities and the havoc they created in my life. They asked me for suggestions on how to survive their own encounters, which led me to dive further into the veil and learn more so I could share it with others in additional paranormal books. Over time, I found myself exploring some nightmarish locations and putting myself in the line of fire in the hopes of learning more about the mysterious paranormal world.

Sam does the same thing. He doesn't simply write about the haunted locations in his book. He also explores them and often has paranormal encounters that defy logic. One such encounter nearly ended his life.

After Sam inadvertently channeled a powerful entity near Salem, he found himself in a sea of uncertainty. His entire personality changed and reality became a blurred line. After I noticed him post several unusual updates online, I reached out to him. The person I began talking to wasn't Sam. Occasionally, the real Sam would emerge from beneath the layers, but it was obvious to me that he wasn't truly himself. Having lived through an extreme attachment myself, I was able to recognize it in Sam.

Convincing him to get help wasn't an easy feat. Because he was under the influence of a powerful presence, he resisted me until I finally wore him down. The results of our experience will soon be documented in the one-hundredth episode of *A Haunting*.

As I write this, I'm packing for my trip to Salem, where we will delve back into the encounter. I'll need to immerse myself in the story and relive those terrifying moments, bringing back memories that I've long suppressed. I'm nervous because I know that every deep dive into the paranormal comes with a price. Sometimes it's a good payoff and I learn something valuable, but other times it comes with a deadly residue that I might never fully shed.

This is what Sam and I endure with every paranormal book. We put ourselves in the middle of some disturbingly dangerous battles so we can document and share our experiences with others. We now have powerful resources such as Michael Robishaw, a shaman who helps us and others like us if we get into trouble. The harsh reality is that we still have to live through those encounters and come out from the other side as unscathed as possible.

This is why I love Sam's concept for *Ghost Writers*. It creates an alliance, one where we can stand stronger together than we ever could apart. I'm certain that Sam and I will join forces again in the future and I look forward to our next adventure.

—Joni Mayhan, author of *Signs of Spirits* and *Ghost Magnet*

INTRODUCTION

Writers have a reputation of being tortured souls languishing among the living. Does the unrest linger in the afterlife?

I've always had an affinity for the ghosts of America's literary past. Having lived in Boston, Florida, and New York City before moving back to Massachusetts twelve years ago, I've had more than a few encounters with the hauntings associated with some of my favorite ghost writers along the way, including Eugene O'Neill, Edgar Allan Poe, Anne Sexton, Charles Dickens, and Nathaniel Hawthorne.

Who needs dead presidents when you're surrounded by a literary spirit squad?

As the author of eleven historical-based ghost books, I've spent years investigating alleged accounts of paranormal activity at sites up and down the East Coast. I've collected a slew of reports from these supposedly haunted locations, and the mission was to give readers a contemporary take on the region's bevy of literati-specific legends.

Ghost Writers is, in essence, a paranormal-themed travel guide written through a historical lens.

Incidentally, I have first-hand experience with several of the haunts in the book. For example, my sophomore-year dormitory at Boston University, the fourth-floor writers' corridor at Shelton Hall now called Kilachand Hall, is rumored to be haunted by Pulitzer Prize winner Eugene O'Neill. Did I have a close encounter with the phantom playwright? Not exactly. But I do remember flickering lights and inexplicable knocks when no one was there. The old hotel's ambiance was eerie and it always exuded a haunted vibe, but I didn't experience anything paranormal.

My first spirited encounter as an adult occurred while I was living in Somerville, Massachusetts, during the early 1990s. I saw an apparition of a young girl who would play hide-and-seek in the hallway near my bedroom. She was a mischievous teen spirit, and I remember hearing phantom footsteps leading up to our second-floor apartment.

Beacon Hill's Acorn Street, known as one of the most-photographed spots in America thanks to its picturesque brownstones and narrow cobblestone lane dating back to the 1820s, is also rumored to be Boston's most haunted. There have been numerous sightings of ghostly, full-bodied apparitions wearing turn-of-the-century and Civil War–era garb passing by the street's ornate, gas-lit lamps. PHOTO COURTESY DEPOSIT PHOTOS.

My personal experiences with the paranormal have been sporadic over the years. I recall spotting a see-through residual spirit of a Confederate soldier when I worked for an alternative newsweekly in Pensacola, Florida. He would appear in the early evening, holding a Civil War–era sword, and pass through the back entrance of the building. It was like a videotaped replay of a traumatic event that occurred years ago.

During my stint in Florida, I also worked as the arts editor of a weekly newspaper for several years and interviewed some of my favorite contemporary authors. In 2006 I chatted with Tabitha King, wife of horror master Stephen and co-author of the gothic-themed book called *Candles Burning*.

I was surprised when King told me that like her famous husband, she doesn't believe in ghosts. "In literature, the ghost is almost always a metaphor for the weight of the past," explained King, phoning from the couple's home in Bangor, Maine. "I don't believe in them in the traditional sense."

I was floored. King has visited some of the most haunted hotels in the country. In fact, the ghosts haunting the Stanley Hotel in Colorado inspired her husband's epic story, *The Shining*.

And, no, King didn't have a "redrum" moment during her stay.

However, she did talk candidly about the dark side of fame and her real-life ghosts—like almost losing her husband after his near-fatal car accident in 1999. "He was in the hospital for twenty-one days," King said. "I told him that he can't have those crises anymore. I can't cope with it emotionally."

When asked if it was difficult finding her own writing voice while being married to an iconic storyteller, she said it wasn't an issue. "We're very different writers and different people," she told me. "We have different needs. I like being anonymous. His notoriety and fame can present serious problems. Most people don't understand that being in the public eye is emotionally exhausting. It takes a lot out of you."

King has seen the dark side of life and it doesn't involve ghosts. "There's a heavy price for fame. It can be a very bad thing," King continued. "But we've been really successful, in many ways, at living a relatively ordinary life. Some of that is because we've stayed in Maine. But, yes, I know how bad—and how extraordinary—it can get."

I had a taste of what King was referring to when I lived in New York City. I was an associate producer and worked on several national television shows for networks under the Viacom umbrella including VH1 and MTV. When I was younger, I remember walking with my friends in the heart of Times Square at night and intuitively knowing I would someday live in the city that never sleeps.

I was smitten with the Big Apple. It was love at first bite.

I moved to Boston in the early nineties for college. When a friend transferred to New York University, she invited me to visit and encouraged me to check out the Washington Square Park parade of freaks during Halloween. It was edgier back then and I remember larger-than-life puppets and furry, four-legged creatures parading through NYC's "haunted corridor."

My friend introduced me to the Village's haunted history. Around the corner from her dorm was where my childhood hero, Edgar Allan Poe, penned the final draft to his narrative classic "The Raven" as well as my favorite tale from that era, "The Cask of the Amontillado." Nowadays, NYU's Furman Hall has taken over the historic 85 West Third Street location. The three-story building where Poe lived for eight months from 1844 to 1845 was torn down in 2001.

All that remains is the façade of his former home and what some say is the Boston-bred icon's ghost. There's a lamppost in front of the allegedly haunted structure and according to the website *Curbed*, "Poe's ghost has been seen climbing it by spooked law students."

Has his spirit been spotted recently? According to multiple sources the answer is, well, "nevermore."

Across West Third Street is another well-documented haunt, Fire Patrol Station No. 2. According to ghost lore, a firehouse phantom with 1930s-era clothing, graying hair, and a mustache roams the building. He's also been spotted wearing firefighting gear and people inside have seen him put on an old-school helmet as if he's suiting up for an alarm. The ghost was identified by a self-proclaimed psychic as Firefighter Schwartz. "He supposedly hanged himself on the fourth floor after he discovered that his wife was being unfaithful," wrote Tom Ogden in *Haunted Greenwich Village*. "This occurred sometime in the decade before World War II—which would explain why his attire dated from that period."

The tall tale snowballed with multiple sightings in the 1990s. One firefighter claimed to have had a face-to-face encounter with the phantom fireman in 1992 saying the ghost leaned over him while he napped on the second floor. Visitors to the structure reported feeling tapped by an unseen force on the spiral staircase, and objects would mysteriously move, like a 150-pound dolly, without explanation.

CNN anchor, Anderson Cooper, purchased the old firehouse in 2009. According to a source who chatted with him, Cooper believes the Firefighter Schwartz ghost story was completely fabricated, and he hasn't had a close encounter with the ghostly mustachioed gent. At least, not yet.

After living in New York City and Florida for eleven years, I moved back to Boston in 2007 and found a first-floor apartment in an old

Victorian-era house in Jamaica Plain. It was only a few blocks from the Forest Hills Cemetery and I would often spend afternoons exploring the historic 275-acre burial ground. During one of my visits, I stumbled on the gravestones of poet e e cummings and my former college roommates, Eugene O'Neill and his wife, Carlotta, but I could not locate the grave marker for which I was looking, that of the Pulitzer Prize–winning poet Anne Sexton, known for her confessional verse and tragic suicide. She was only forty-six when she died and I understood she was ultimately interred in Forest Hills.

Determined, I created dowsing rods from wire hangers I found in my closet. Today I own a pair of "witch sticks" crafted by a Salem high priestess that are more elaborate, but this hack worked. With my makeshift rods leading the way, I discovered Sexton's grave hidden by a copse of trees.

Did I see her ghost? No. But my spirit communication with her did inspire me to revisit her work. At the time I didn't know she was friends with one of my other favorite female writers from that era, Sylvia Plath. *The Bell Jar* author met Sexton at a writing workshop taught by Robert Lowell in 1958. They reportedly became fast friends and would meet at Boston's Ritz-Carlton for a post-class gathering, downing dry martinis.

Sadly, both women committed suicide. Plath was found with her head in an oven on February 11, 1963. She reportedly died from gas poisoning. Sexton, less than a dozen years after her friend passed, ended her life in the garage of her suburban home in Weston, Massachusetts, on October 4, 1974.

What did I get from my journey of self-discovery in search of Sexton's grave? History repeats itself, and it was my job to give a voice to those without a voice—even though most of the stories turned out to be tales from the crypt.

It wasn't my last graveyard epiphany.

While researching a Halloween-themed story for a local magazine, I started spending hours in the Boston Common. I've always felt a strong magnetic pull to the site of the Great Elm, also known as the hanging tree. I also had an inexplicable interest in the Central Burying Ground. One night while walking by the old cemetery, I noticed a young female figure wearing what looked like a hospital gown and standing by a tree. In an instant she was gone.

A few months after the incident I joined a group of tour guides who specialize in telling Boston's paranormal history and I learned about many of the ghosts from New England's blood-stained closet. Over the years I had stayed away from the Omni Park House hotel because it had a mysterious vibe to it, but while giving tours, I had several encounters with the paranormal there. On one such occasion, while taking a photo in front of the famed "enchanted mirror" on the hotel's second-floor mezzanine, I noticed condensation mysteriously appear on the mirror as if someone, or something, was breathing on it. According to hotel lore, the antique mirror was taken from Charles Dickens's room, and he apparently stood in front of it to practice his nineteenth-century orations. Perhaps he still was? While the ghost story is intriguing, what interested me more was that the press room next to the creepy mirror is where John F. Kennedy announced his candidacy for president. I've seen tons of photos and heard many stories from guests who had strange encounters while staying on the hotel's upper floors, and today the Omni Parker House has become one of my favorite hot spots in the city. Haunted history oozes from the oldest continuously operating hotel in the country.

In addition to giving tours in Boston, I've also written two books on Salem and spent a lot of time at the Turner-Ingersoll Mansion, inspiration for Nathaniel Hawthorne's *The House of the Seven Gables*. While researching my book *Wicked Salem: Exploring Lingering Lore and Legends*, I signed up to give tours at The Gables in October 2017 so I could check out the location for myself. But, after giving dozens of tours during the museum's busy season, I never had a paranormal experience there. Oddly it was during a tour led by a fellow guide in April 2018 that I had a haunted encounter in the museum's attic. I felt as if someone, or something, was tugging on my shirt as if trying to get my attention. Was it a ghost child? Yes, I'm sure of it.

While I'm not convinced that the rest of the house is actually haunted, I can say without hesitation that the other historical structures on campus—including Hawthorne's birthplace, the Hooper-Hathaway House, and the Retire-Beckett house—are paranormally active.

Author Sam Baltrusis investigated many of the haunted locations featured in Ghost Writers. PHOTO BY FRANK C. GRACE.

One day after giving tours, I was clocking out in the Hooper-Hathaway house and the door literally slammed in my face. I then heard a female voice say "stay." I noticed my jacket was somehow stuck in the door handle. I had to ask a coworker to help me untangle my sleeve so I could leave the historic structure built in 1682.

During a visit at the Retire-Beckett house, which is home to the gift shop, I was looking for a copy of my book, *Ghosts of Salem*, for a guest on my tour. After looking through the stacks, I watched in awe as my book literally flew off the shelf and landed on the floor in front of me.

Of course, not all of my paranormal experiences involved ghost writers as legendary as Hawthorne. While doing last-minute research for my book on haunted hotels over Labor Day weekend in 2017, I hopped on the Downeaster Amtrak leaving from Boston's North Station en route to Southern Maine. I had let the ghosts guide me to this rustic Maine haunt after pulling The Kennebunk Inn from a hat chock-full of potential haunted hotels. I had no idea that the ghost of poet Silas H. Perkins would greet me when I walked into the historic hotel.

As far as the paranormal activity at the inn, I encountered more than one spirit during the overnight stay. I recorded my experiences online and several psychic mediums claimed to have seen a balding man follow me all over the house. A male energy with a thin stature and a child spirit also made themselves felt. In my room on the second floor, I picked up two words on a ghost-hunting tool called an Ovilus. The device mysteriously spit out "poem" and "read."

Perkins—whose poem "The Common Road" was syndicated nationally from the funeral train of President Franklin Roosevelt—responded when I read his words out loud. I captured on my recorder what sounded like footsteps moving closer to me on the wooden floor, which are unusually creaky, followed by a disembodied male voice. At first I panicked when I felt the spirit next to me, and then the ghost poet walked away.

Of course not all the places I've visited with a rich literary tradition are haunted by former wordsmiths. Of all the locations I visited while researching *Ghost Writers*, there was one haunt that should be a postmortem hangout teeming with the spirits of America's long-gone authors, but

The attic of the Turner-Ingersoll Mansion in Salem, Massachusetts, inspired author Nathaniel Hawthorne's *The House of the Seven Gables*.
PHOTO BY FRANK C. GRACE.

it's not. Contrary to expectations, Sleepy Hollow Cemetery in Concord, Massachusetts, isn't haunted by its famous-but-dead inhabitants.

Within Sleepy Hollow Cemetery, Authors Ridge is the final resting spot for some of New England's top ghost writers including Henry David Thoreau, Louisa May Alcott, Nathaniel Hawthorne, and Ralph Waldo Emerson. Designed in the early nineteenth century, the graveyard was intentionally created as a "garden of the living" to encourage visitors to enjoy the picturesque scenery while honoring the departed.

There is one alleged haunting at Sleepy Hollow Cemetery involving the eerie grave of Ephraim Bull. He wasn't a writer, but the visionary was the first to cultivate the Concord grape. Apparently, Bull was a bitter man when he died because he never saw any profits from the fruits of his life-long work. His tomb is inscribed with: "He sowed, others reaped." If it's true that there is postmortem unrest associated with unfinished business,

Authors Ridge in Sleepy Hollow Cemetery is the final resting place of several legendary writers and transcendentalists who once lived in the city of Concord, Massachusetts. PHOTO BY SAM BALTRUSIS.

Bull's spirit probably does linger among the skeletal remains of America's elite nineteenth-century writers in Concord.

While standing in the middle of Authors Ridge, I had the ultimate realization. If the ghost writers featured in this book were tortured souls when they were alive, will the unrest continue in the afterlife? Based on my research and actual face-to-face encounters with the ghosts of America's literary past, all signs point to "yes."

And that's how the story begins.

GHOST PROFILE: JOHN ZAFFIS

"If the day ever comes when John Zaffis doesn't fear anything, it's time for me to get the hell out of this line of work."
—John Zaffis, *Haunted Collector*

John Zaffis, star of the *Haunted Collector* and co-author of *Demon Haunted*, has been called every name in the book. "I've heard Ziggity, old man, gray beard, you name it," Zaffis joked during a recent interview. "You've never heard of Ziggity? People call me that all the time."

The latest nickname making the rounds is the "godfather of the paranormal" and he's not exactly sure how that one came about. "There are so many," he told me. "I believe it started when one of my agents called me the 'godfather of the paranormal' and it just kind of stuck. I went with it."

Zaffis said the "godfather" moniker was an upgrade compared to what people nicknamed him back in the day when he first started investigating with his famous uncle and aunt, Ed and Lorraine Warren. "People would call me the 'paranormal brat' because I would always run to my Uncle Ed if I had a problem," he recalled.

Nowadays, up-and-coming investigators in the paranormal field reach out to *him* for advice. Armed with more than forty-six years of experience, Zaffis tends to be the voice of reason during an inves-

PHOTO COURTESY JOHN ZAFFIS.

tigation. "The thing I do more so now than before is if I'm having a paranormal experience, I don't say anything," he explained. "I wait for someone around me to say something because that verifies that it's not my imagination. When other people start validating what I'm sensing at a haunted location, that's what I use as my gauge."

Of course, Zaffis still makes the occasional rookie mistake. When he was dealing with a possession case, for example, he had a knee-jerk reaction when he saw a woman levitating in front of him. "My first instinct was to push her down," he said. "And I did."

In addition to experiencing an entity-induced levitation, the demonologist has seen all sorts of extreme paranormal activity over the years. In fact, Zaffis has worked with well-known exorcists such as Bishop Robert McKenna and Malachi Martin. "One time, I witnessed a person who was truly possessed," he said. "He wasn't thrashing around while he was going through the rites of exorcism."

Zaffis said he did see something that truly terrified him during the possession however. "[The man] opened his eyes and they were reptilian. That really took me back. The intensity was so high with that particular demon, it didn't need to do anything to prove itself or to manifest."

The co-author of *Demon Haunted* had to decompress for a few days so he could process the horror that unfolded in front of him. "In the heat of the moment, I'm not the one to react," he explained. "I'm usually even-keeled and then realize the severity of the situation much later."

While he tries to keep calm during intense situations, Zaffis said he's learned from his mistakes. "It's trial and error," he explained. "I often share my experiences because even people like John Zaffis have had their back up against the wall from time to time. It's key that you share what you've experienced so that others can benefit from the knowledge."

Based on his experiences as the lead investigator featured on the *Haunted Collector*, Zaffis knows a thing or two about enchanted objects. "I put items in the same category as haunted land and places. If an item is haunted it doesn't necessarily mean there's something evil attached to it. In some situations, there's an energy associated with the item and it's not always bad."

Zaffis stores the haunted objects he's picked up along the way in a barn outside of his Connecticut home. He also has a procedure to bind his collection that includes prayer, sea salt, and holy water.

"If people randomly collect haunted items, it's not a good idea to keep them in their personal space," he said. "I'm not interested in playing Russian roulette. I rather keep them in a separate building."

As someone who has been on television and has worked with most of the well-known investigators in the field, Zaffis said he doesn't always trust what airs on the small screen. "Are a lot of these things on TV done for entertainment value? Yes, absolutely."

Zaffis said what happens in front of the camera is more about keeping people interested and less about actually finding answers. However, it doesn't mean they're not trying. "We are all on a journey and searching," he told me. "At the end of the day, can we prove or disprove that there's a heaven or a hell? None of us really know. We don't have the hardcore evidence we need from a scientific perspective. That's one of the driving forces for many of us. We still can't prove or disprove these things we've experienced."

The "godfather of the paranormal" has noticed a dramatic shift in pop culture thanks to a post-*Conjuring* interest in the Warrens and television shows such as the *Haunted Collector*. "People look at the paranormal differently now because of the amount of exposure on TV, radio, and conventions," he said. "They have a different perspective. What I mean by that is that they realize there's something that transpires beyond the physical body. There's just too much out there we can't explain."

When I asked Zaffis about the backlash his aunt and uncle faced during the Amityville case, he said he believes it was a fear-based attack. "Back in the day, who else was out there? It was such a small community," he said. "Those two would push more doors open than anybody else in the field. No one would take that chance. They did. They broke down barriers. They took a beating, but they stood their ground."

Ed Warren passed away on August 23, 2006, and I asked Zaffis what he thought his uncle would think about the paranormal now. "The one thing that bothers me is that he wasn't around to see the success of *The Conjuring* or to see the paranormal finally come to the forefront," he said.

Sadly, his aunt Lorraine passed on April 18, 2019. She was ninety-two.

Even though more people are accepting that spirits and demons are real, Zaffis does bump into the occasional non-believer. "If someone is a skeptic, I really don't take offense," he said.

"Even though I grew up surrounded by the paranormal, I didn't believe in ghosts until I was sixteen years old. When I was going to bed one night, I saw a transparent, tall figure that was shaking his head back and forth."

When he told his mother about the incident, Zaffis learned that when his grandfather was alive, he always shook his head when he was upset. A few days after the close encounter, his grandmother passed. Fueled by the life-changing experience, Zaffis became interested in the paranormal and spent his formative years studying under the Warrens.

Zaffis told me that he keeps an open mind when it comes to his work out in the field. "If someone is scratched, it doesn't always mean we're dealing with something demonic," he explained. "I used to think that if a person got pushed or scratched, that it was something evil. Not necessarily. I look at it differently today. If a person was a mean, rotten person when they were alive, then they will be like that in spirit form."

However, if a case does involve a demonic infestation, Zaffis protects himself on a spiritual level. "A demonologist is a person who studies across the board and looks at the different belief systems and organized religions out there. Looking at the hardcore stuff on the occult level, my guard remains very high, but I'm respectful and try to understand where they are coming from when I approach a case."

When he works on the hardcore cases, Zaffis tries to keep his family and his work completely separate. "I live a dual life if that makes any sense," he said. "Sometimes being involved with the heavier stuff can be very isolating. You have to discipline yourself and know where you have to draw the line when dealing with the paranormal and your family life."

Zaffis, who runs the Paranormal and Demonology Research Society of New England, said his uncle taught him how to find balance. "He always told me, 'You have to live in two different worlds, Kid.' As time went on, I understood what he meant," Zaffis said. "There's a lot of work I get involved with that will probably go to the grave with me. I just don't talk about those cases. I learned that from both Ed and Lorraine. There are things you simply need to leave alone."

As a practicing Roman Catholic, Zaffis said it's important for him to help people find some sort of normalcy in their lives after surviving an extreme haunting. "If someone is levitating, I don't look at it like I did ten or twenty years ago," he said. "Back then, I would have grabbed a camcorder. Now, I want to help these people."

While Zaffis has pretty much seen it all, he still proceeds with caution when he investigates. "If the day ever comes when John Zaffis doesn't fear anything, it's time for me to get the hell out of this line of work," he concluded.

GHOST ENCOUNTER:
BRIGHT LIGHTS, HAUNTED CITY

"Sometimes you have to confront your darkest fears head on. For me, the ghosts of my past during my stint in NYC wouldn't let me go."

—Sam Baltrusis, author of *Ghost Writers*

I see dead people. And, in one disturbing nightmare that was recently featured on the television show *A Haunting*, I've been possessed by them.

It went down at a place I thought was safe. The event was called the Haunting at Witch Hill and I was asked to tell spooky stories wearing Victorian-era garb at the historic Peirce Farm in Topsfield, Massachusetts, the night before Halloween in 2016. I decided to retell the story of the so-called "crime of the century" that riveted Salem in 1830 and involved a black sheep family member of one of the structure's former owners. A man by the name of Richard Crowninshield had been hired by relatives of Captain Joseph White, an eighty-two-year-old shipmaster and trader, to murder him. He snuck into the captain's house one night and killed the older man by whacking him over the head with a twenty-two-inch piece of refurbished hickory known as an "Indian club," and stabbing him thirteen times with a dirk near his heart.

After an extremely draining October giving tours in Salem and managing the paranormal experience at a haunted attraction called Ghost Ship Harbor, I thought the evening went off rather well. Visitors seemed to enjoy my retelling of the sensational case that was rumored to have inspired ghost writers Edgar Allan Poe and Nathaniel Hawthorne.

After the event, however, I began to feel both spiritually and mentally off-kilter. It felt like I was surrounded by a cloud of frustration, but I wasn't really sure what was happening. I reached out to the paranormal community for help. I called my friend Joni Mayhan and she grew concerned about my behavior. She could tell I was not myself. She consulted her shaman contact, Michael Robishaw, who was able to help me identify what was happening.

I had somehow picked up an attachment, or a disembodied entity that attached itself to my energy field. "The entity attached to you is a male, around twenty-six-years old when he was killed," the shaman told me. "He has anxiety issues and is not happy at all. He likes to be loud and very obnoxious. He comes from a wealthy family."

Thinking back over past events, I knew exactly what attached itself to me, and when. It was during the event at Peirce Farm and my attachment was none other than the disgruntled spirit of Richard Crowninshield, the crime-for-hire murderer of Captain Joseph White. He came from a wealthy family and, by most accounts, was loud and obnoxious.

What was interesting was the fact that Robishaw said Crowninshield was "killed," when by all accounts the man had committed suicide in his jail cell before being convicted. This raised an investigative red flag with me and confirmed my reading at Peirce Farm at Witch Hill. Crowninshield told me during the channeling session that he didn't commit suicide in prison and that he may have been murdered in 1830.

Another freakish thing I uncovered and didn't know at the time? The fact that Crowninshield was twenty-six years old when he died in prison. Robishaw nailed it.

Thankfully, Robishaw was also able to "bind and banish" the attachment.

Nick Groff, a pop-culture investigator formerly from Destination America's *Paranormal Lockdown,* talked about his experiences with negative spirit attachments in a previous interview. "Positive and negative energies really do exist and they can have a major effect on you and your well-being," Groff told me. "If something is going to attach itself to me after leaving a negative location, it's difficult to get rid of that energy when you go home. Mentally, I try to stay strong and eventually it depreciates. It goes away."

"Sometimes certain situations take longer than others," he continued. "But I try to close the door when I leave a location. I just block it out. If you don't, it tends to feed on negativity, and it intensifies when you go home."

I was glad to have been freed of my murderous attachment. Later, I learned that my friend Jack Kenna, a paranormal investigator from the television shows *Haunted Case Files* and *Paranormal Survivor*, encountered an entity he also believes to be the accused murderer. Apparently, Crowninshield gets around.

For the record, the possession by Crowninshield wasn't my only trip to the attachment rodeo. I had an encounter with a negative entity while living in New York City during the summer of 2000. I was walking from my job on Broadway to my apartment in the East Village and I had a close encounter with something inexplicable that has haunted me for years.

It felt like the frigid hand of death grabbing my ankle.

I was casually walking through Washington Square Park, a trek I had made hundreds of times, and I clearly remember feeling something touch my ankle. I looked down thinking someone was pulling a practical joke or a homeless person was hiding in the flower bed and trying to get my attention. No one was there.

I kept walking and then I felt it again. The second time was more profound, as the disembodied hand frantically held on. I had to physically reach down and try to knock off the death grip of someone who was definitely not there.

I didn't tell a soul. I thought it was something explainable. Then it happened again.

It was a particularly warm winter day a few months later when I was walking right around the same spot, the corner of Washington Square Park East. I felt the mysterious hand again, and this time it wasn't letting go.

I didn't even think about the possibility of it being a ghost. At this point in my life I was wearing what I call "paranormal blinders" and quickly tried to shrug off the incident.

In hindsight, I believe the spirit was desperately trying to tell me something. Or worse, it was trying to attach itself to me.

Joni Mayhan, author of *Dark and Scary Things*, told me that it's possible the entity I encountered at Washington Square Park was preying on my sensitivity to the paranormal. "I've had a few really horrible attachments," explained Mayhan. "One of them was the subject of my book, *Soul Collector*."

Mayhan said sensitives are like beacons of light to the spirit realm. "Since everybody senses them differently, it's always difficult to say if you had an attachment or not. One big sign, though, is a personality change or sudden depression. Dark moods and a feeling of just not wanting to live anymore are pretty common. They don't have to touch us to attach to us, but it probably makes it easier if they do. They've penetrated our shield."

After the second encounter in Washington Square Park, my mood did change. In fact, I was overwhelmed by negativity. I mysteriously started having issues with anxiety and would drink alcohol to self-medicate. It was as if the icy hand of death had pulled me into the abyss. I was drowning with negative emotions and my life started to spiral out of control.

"Investigators often flock to haunted venues, needlessly paying tremendous amounts of money to hunt for a ghost, while passing several dozen ghosts on their way to the door. Ghosts are everywhere," Mayhan continued. "You'll find them lurking in places where you find groups of people. Shopping malls and movie theaters are prime locations, as are restaurants, hospitals, and churches. Most of the time the ghosts are happy to remain there, but occasionally they find one human they feel is worth following."

I believe this is what happened to me in New York. The entity had attached itself to me and was feeding off my energy, and the experience almost destroyed me. After a series of traumatic events, including a violent mugging on a subway platform, and then the horrific devastation of 9/11, I became a shell of my former self in the months after my encounter in Washington Square Park. After intensive therapy and then years of sobriety in Boston, I was in a better mental place. But it had not been easy.

I've mentioned this encounter at various book signings, including a speaking engagement at the Massachusetts State House. When one of the guests at the event mentioned to me that the skeletal remains of hundreds of bodies were uncovered in Washington Square Park, I couldn't breathe.

Sometimes you have to confront your darkest fears head on. For me, the ghosts of my past during my stint in New York wouldn't let me go. I had to see for myself if the unmarked graves buried beneath the park were related to the disembodied hand I felt on my ankle in 2000. I needed closure. It was time.

Photographer Jason Baker joined me on this journey to revisit some of the most haunted locations in my former hometown. In hindsight, we did have some truly creepy experiences along the way, including being chased on Roosevelt Island by an army of squirrels in front of the smallpox hospital, exploring the lingering energy at Sailors' Snug Harbor, and a spirited overnight stay at the allegedly haunted Jane Hotel on the extreme West End of Manhattan.

The hotel's lobby looked like something from the set of *American Horror Story: Hotel*. In fact, I expected Lady Gaga to pop up from behind the check-in counter when I rang the bell. The doorman was wearing an old-school uniform and the vibe was *The*

Grand Budapest Hotel with a touch of *The Shining*. My ears started to ring, which is usually a telltale sign that a location is haunted.

Apparently, my reputation as a ghost writer had somehow preceded my visit. "Are you a sensitive?" asked Kitty, the hotel's front-desk concierge. "Maybe you can tell us if it's haunted. I haven't had an experience personally, but I have heard all sorts of stories about people encountering ghosts here. There's one story I've heard several times of a spirit without clothes walking in the lobby and out of the door."

Naked ghosts? Been there, done that. However, I wanted to dig into the hotel's backstory to figure out why it would be paranormally active.

Opened in 1908 by the American Seamen's Friend Society, the hotel boasted 156 rooms for the captains and employees of the luxury cruise ships of the day. According to the *New York Times,* "The officers had rooms similar to those in a hotel, but the rooms for sailors, about seven by seven feet, were strung out along two narrow corridors, like berths on a yacht. In 1912, survivors of the *Titanic* were sheltered there. More than one hundred of them gathered one night for a memorial service at which they sang 'Nearer, My God, to Thee.' The sailors were destitute, their pay having stopped the day the *Titanic* sank, and people left money and clothes for them at the building."

Reportedly, those sailors were not the only occupants from the *Titanic* who found refuge at the Jane Hotel; the hotel is supposedly haunted by the "doomed souls that had not made it," wrote Dr. Philip Schoenberg in *Ghosts of Manhattan.* "Since then, elevators have arrived unsummoned, cold spots have been experienced in different locations of the hotel, and moans and groans have been heard in certain rooms."

After a sleepless night in our excruciatingly small, bunk-bed room, Baker left early to take the hard-hat tour of what remained of the Ellis Island Hospital complex while I tried to sneak in a few hours of sleep.

Did I have a paranormal experience at the Jane Hotel other than the ear ringing? No. However, I did have a dream involving magician Harry Houdini. The legendary escape artist lived in a beautiful townhouse located at 278 West 113th Street in Harlem from 1904 to his tragic death in 1926. Maybe I was picking up on Houdini's lingering energy in the city that never sleeps.

Baker was visibly shaken when we met up on the Staten Island ferry after his tour. "There was something about that hospital that made me physically ill," he told me. "It seriously made me sick." Hundreds of immigrants were kept in the hospital complex because of ailments such as tuberculosis and the measles. In addition to the quarantine wards, the infirmary was a literal dumping ground for pregnant women and the mentally ill. Baker was probably picking up on the psychic imprint left behind.

After he recovered from his tour of the Ellis Island hospital, we ventured out to Sailors' Snug Harbor. Opened in 1833, this Staten Island campus of five Greek Revival–style buildings served as the country's first home for retired merchant seaman. As far as the legends associated with the complex, a matron was allegedly murdered in a cottage on the campus by her illegitimate son. The boy was rumored to be a hanged as punishment. Of course, there's no proof of this legend. The Matron's Cottage is reportedly haunted, with doors opening and closing by themselves and a chair kept in the basement rattling without provocation.

While the matron story was probably fabricated, there was a documented murder-suicide that happened at Sailors' Snug Harbor on January 30, 1863. A resident named Herman Ingalls shot the Reverend Robert Quinn with a double-barrel pistol outside of the Snug Harbor chapel at 9:00 a.m. "You'll expose me. I know you will, if you live," said Ingalls, according to the *New York Times*. Quinn was shot near his heart and died yelling, "I'm shot! I'm shot!" Ingalls then pointed the pistol at his own head and pulled the trigger. The sailor, losing his entire lower jaw in the suicide attempt, died in the hospital later that night.

I chatted with an employee, Hillary, manning the front desk at the visitor's center. When I asked her if she thought Sailors' Snug Harbor was haunted, she sheepishly nodded. "I'm here by myself a lot and you see shadows at the corner of your eye. You also get phantom smells from time to time," she told me. As far as the legend associated with the matron, the tour guide said that it's probably not true. "There were a bunch of women-loving guys here," she said. "When a woman was here, they gathered around her."

Hillary said she had an experience that could be viewed as paranormal. One afternoon, she was playing the piano in the visitor's center and she distinctly heard a male voice say, "Shhh." Was she scared? "No, not really," she told me. "The ghosts here are benevolent. If you tell them to stop, they do."

As far as my paranormal experiences at Sailors' Snug Harbor, I did pick up words like "bet," and "child" on my Ovilus. One odd incident involved a group of boys playing cops and robbers near the music hall. When I was standing at the exact location where Ingalls murdered Reverend Quinn, a boy playfully pretended to shoot me with his plastic gun. Was it paranormal? No. But it was definitely a bizarre moment of serendipity.

Speaking of strange twists, Sailors' Snug Harbor earned national ink in 2018 when multiple grave markers of the retired "Snugs" who lived and died at the facility were discovered in the bowels of the complex. "More than one-hundred-year-old limestone headstones are rotting in the basement of a building on the waterfront campus of Snug Harbor Cultural Center, lifted decades ago from a cemetery containing the remains of seven thousand old salts who died between 1833 and 1975 when the complex housed retired sailors," reported the *New York Post* on June 30, 2018. "The tombstones were removed to protect them from vandals, but now no one knows where the dead are buried."

Based on years of experience as a paranormal researcher, I understand that it's common for ghosts to become unhinged in the

The Matron's Cottage at Sailors' Snug Harbor in Staten Island was investigated by the Travel Channel's Ghost Adventures. PHOTO BY JASON BAKER.

afterlife if their grave markers are desecrated or their final resting place is unkempt. Perhaps the salty specters are haunting Sailors' Snug Harbor in search of their skeletal remains?

After our brief-but-memorable visit to Snug Harbor, Baker and I decided to check out Roosevelt Island before heading to the dead man dumping ground in Washington Square Park. I had no idea that we were about to face a pack of killer squirrels.

"We're not supposed to talk about the ghosts," said Francine Lange, a volunteer who manned the historical society kiosk near the Roosevelt Island Tramway. "Horrible things happened here, so I wouldn't be surprised if some of that bad mojo is still on the island." The visitor center kiosk had a few items for sale, including an "Asylum for the Insane" coffee mug and a cute squirrel stuffed animal that oddly foreshadowed our two-mile journey across what was originally known as Blackwell's Island.

Lange did a great job of directing us to the must-see hot spots. However, she should have warned us about the blood-thirsty squirrels waiting for us on the extreme tip of the island. At first, the four-legged creatures seemed harmless, but the scene quickly turned dark.

Located on New York's Staten Island, Sailors' Snug Harbor is a National Historic Landmark District made up of twenty-six buildings arranged within an eighty-three-acre city park. PHOTO BY JASON BAKER.

Ghosts usually don't scare me. Neither do animals. However, the army of squirrels attacking Baker and myself outside of the abandoned smallpox hospital, also known as Renwick Ruin, on Roosevelt Island genuinely creeped me out.

At first, we were approached by what seemed like a friendly squirrel. Then a crew of his critter friends approached us. It started to turn scary when the pack of squirrels followed us around the smallpox hospital. We started to run and they literally chased us off of the southern tip of the island. Yes, it was like a scene from an Alfred Hitchcock movie.

It was almost as if the ravenous animals were protecting the lost souls of the 13,000 people who died from smallpox there in the 1800s. Spirited sentinel squirrels? Yep, only in New York.

Renwick had one-hundred beds and opened in 1856. Thousands died there at the height of the smallpox outbreak. "Corpses would be stacked at the end of each floor, burned, and then dumped into the East River," reported Nicholas Parco from the *New York Daily News*. Renwick shut down in 1875 and then became a nursing school for the employees of nearby Charity Hospital. The gothic-style structure was abandoned in the 1950s and was later gutted by a fire. It was also a notorious hangout for drug addicts.

"Back then it was fully structured," a park ranger named Osborne had told Parco. "A lot of people used to use drugs in there."

An older female spirit wearing a soiled hospital gown has been spotted walking the grounds near the Renwick Ruin. "People say they hear ghosts," Osborne had continued. "I don't think so."

The next stop on our self-guided tour of Roosevelt Island was the Octagon, a luxury condo that had a past life as the New York City Lunatic Asylum from 1841 until 1894. Charles Dickens was unnerved by the hospital's inhumane conditions when he toured the facility in 1842. "Everything had a lounging, listless, madhouse air, which was very painful," Dickens said.

Nellie Bly was equally horrified during her short stint in the women's wing of the asylum during the 1880s. In fact, her book *Ten Days in a Mad-House* challenged the mental healthcare system in America. "The insane asylum on Blackwell's Island is a human rat-trap," Bly wrote in 1887. "It is easy to get in, but once there it is impossible to get out."

As far as hauntings, residents of the Octagon claim that there is a lingering residual energy that has psychically imprinted itself

Renwick Ruin was a former smallpox hospital located on Roosevelt Island in New York City. PHOTO BY JASON BAKER.

into the structure's blue-gray stone that was quarried on the island. "If you care about ghost stories, you may not want to live here," said Octagon resident Li Li to the *Daily News*.

After our quick walkthrough of the Octagon, Baker and I headed to the one spot in Manhattan that had haunted me for years. Washington Square Park was where I picked up my first attachment in 2000. What scared me the most? I was terrified it would happen again.

I spent the summer of 1993 at the NYU dorm on Third Avenue while interning at *Seventeen* magazine. I spent many afternoons in Washington Square Park, reading and jotting down observations in my notebook. One line I wrote still haunts me: "This is where the dead people go." I'm not sure what I was referring to, but I did feel a magnetic force summon me back to this spot day after day.

Finding out years later that more than 20,000 people were buried in the park—an estimate that includes burials from the Native American Sapokanikan tribe coupled with victims from the yellow fever epidemic from 1791 to 1821.

"Washington Square Park became a public park in 1827," reported the online source *Curbed*. "The park, located in the Village and surrounded by NYU, was once home to a graveyard. In 1797 the land was acquired by the Common Council for use as a potter's field and a place for public executions. Some historians think that the land might also have been used as a cemetery for one of the adjacent churches, as headstones have been unearthed in the park."

When I returned to my old stomping grounds in November 2015, the rumored skeletal remains from a hidden burial vault at the corner of Washington Square Park East and Waverly Place were uncovered while crews were updating the city's century-old water main system. "We're hoping now to confirm what the descendent church might be," said Alyssa Loorya, president of Chrysalis Archaeological Consultants, adding that the vaults date back to the late 1700s up to the early eighteenth century. "You normally don't find burial vaults beneath the city streets."

Based on the city's policy, crews had to leave the skeletal remains as they found them. Returning to the scene, you could see what looked like bones from the exposed vaults covered by pieces of plywood.

While walking past these death pits with Baker, I had the sensation of an energy passing through my body for just a second and then quickly leave. It was a familiar tingling feeling. "Something just passed through me," I said. There was a jolt of electricity and then I felt drained, shivering in the beauty and the madness of the moment.

According to Mayhan, "Ghosts will pull energy where they can find it. A typical sign that a ghost is using your energy is the sensation of vibration. When they pull energy from us, sometimes their vibrational rate is different from ours, giving us the feeling that we are vibrating from the inside out."

I looked up at the Washington Square arch. To the right was a larger-than-life moon, only a few days after the last full one before the winter solstice. Native Americans called it the "moon when deer shed antlers." It's also known as the "mourning moon."

At this point, I decided to let go and accept that I have an ability that's both a blessing and a curse. I'm clairvoyant. I see dead people and it's my job as an author to chronicle the stories of the spirits I encounter along the way.

I took a deep breath and slowly exhaled. "The ghosts of my past will no longer haunt me," I said out loud. No more fear.

THE REBELS

"Invisible things are the only realities."

—EDGAR ALLAN POE, *LOSS OF BREATH*

GHOST PROFILE: J.W. OCKER

"One of the reasons that Poe's legacy has survived is because he's universal. Poe was really not of this place."

—J.W. Ocker, *Poe-Land*

The lingering legacy surrounding Edgar Allan Poe still doesn't make any sense to *Poe-Land* author J.W. Ocker. It's an oddity that continues to saturate pop culture with images of creepy black birds and sad-sack smirks from a penniless writer who died more than a 170 years ago.

For Ocker, Poe's status as a literary and cultural icon is one giant, Gothic-style question mark. Know Poe? Not exactly.

"It blew my mind," the *Poe-Land* author told me. "He's still so relevant and he shouldn't be. It fascinated me that you can buy an action figure of Poe. I mean, there's an NFL football team named after one of his poems and he's even a Halloween decoration. No other poet could have that. Only Poe could pull that off."

Even after writing his award-winning travelogue on the man who penned the first, modern whodunit, "The Murders at the Rue Morgue," Ocker still doesn't completely know Poe.

"I couldn't figure him out," Ocker continued. "If you dig deeper, however, you start to realize that he was the fount of many

PHOTO COURTESY J.W. OCKER.

30

of our modern stories. He invented the detective genre. He pushed science fiction ahead of its time. He Americanized horror and gave us a voice. Before we were ghosts and tassels. Now, we have maniacs with axes. Even today, the story of killers chopping up bodies and hiding them is still an active part of the American horror trope."

Ocker said his fascination with Poe started in childhood and eventually inspired him to write his *Grimpendium* book series as well as content for his website called *OTIS: Odd Things I've Seen.* "I've always been a fan of Poe," he said. "Even before I was really into literature, I remember making myself memorize 'The Raven' for no apparent reason. As I grew older, Poe was always around on TV. There were movies about him and he was on t-shirts. Poe wasn't a dead author like the others you study in school. He's an active part of popular culture."

Ocker was determined to pen a book on Poe but wanted to do something completely different. Why not follow in the footsteps of the father of American horror fiction and write about it? "As someone who is in the oddity business, there's a lot of Poe still around like houses and objects," Ocker explained. "There were literally pieces of him, like in his coffin, still around. There are a million books on him but no one has done this type of book before."

When Ocker first started the research for *Poe-Land,* he headed to the poet's original stomping grounds in Boston, Massachusetts. "There's a whole cult of Poe that I didn't know about. There's this group of Poe fans who actively keep him alive, like the people who run museums as well as collectors and performers," Ocker explained. "When I started the book, I had no names. I knew there was a guy in Massachusetts who was responsible for putting up the plaque across from Boston Common. Norman George, who's deceased now, opened me up to this whole cult of Poe that I didn't know existed."

As far as Poe's relationship with his hometown, Ocker said that his animosity was misdirected. "If you just read his works and don't know his history, he seemed to be really against Boston," he told me. "Poe hated transcendental poetry and Boston was the center of that movement. Poe strongly disliked their style of writing and they were all getting really famous. If you read between the lines, Poe was jealous. All of those insults were on paper but his anti-Boston jabs were directed toward the transcendentalists."

On October 16, 1845, there was the legendary Boston Lyceum incident, where Poe was expected to read "The Raven" but opted to orate his lesser-known "Al Araaf" poem, which caused a backlash in Boston. He retaliated by calling Bostonians "Frogpondians," alluding to the Frog Pond wading pool in Boston Common, and mocked transcendentalist writers in New England like Ralph Waldo Emerson and Margaret Fuller.

"The story is that he hated Boston and Boston hated him back," Ocker continued. "In response, the city never claimed him as a native son. It's a great story but I don't think it's true. Boston has a wealth of things to be famous for like medicine, sports, and politics. It's easy to lose a gem like Poe."

Rejection was a recurring theme in Poe's life, Ocker said. "Deep down, I believe, Poe loved Boston," he noted. "And he wanted Boston to love him back."

When it comes to Poe's public personae and his topsy-turvy life as a tortured writer, Ocker said he's often misunderstood. "As a person, Poe was less complex," he explained. "Poe wanted to do great things as an author. His poverty defined him. He had higher standards than his lifestyle allowed. He was always a guy looking for a family and a home. He wanted fame and a piece of land that was his own. He never got any of that during his lifetime."

According to Ocker, there was an incident at the Providence Athenaeum that could have left a psychic imprint. Poe was jilted romantically by a fellow poet, Sarah Helen Whitman.

"He knew her from the writing business," Ocker explained. "Sarah Helen Whitman had money, which was something Poe never had. Of course, some people assumed that her money was his motivation for the relationship. He would come to Providence regularly to woo her, but her mom didn't like him. At one point he had to promise not to drink anymore to marry her, which was a promise that he broke."

Ocker said one of the places the couple would regularly hang out was at the Providence Athenaeum. During one romantic tête-à-tête, Whitman showed Poe a poem called "Ulalume," published anonymously in the December 1847 edition of the *American Whig Review*. Poe revealed himself as the author and signed his name in pencil next to the poem.

"It was a nice date move," Ocker joked. "He regularly published things anonymously. He then signed the poem for her and put it back in the stacks. At some point after his death, Whitman told the library and they found it. The signed poem is stored in their special collections and it's sometimes put on display."

Whitman, based on her later-in-life recollections, received an anonymous letter stating that Poe had broken his vow to her to stay sober, directly leading to an end of the relationship.

Soon after their breakup, Poe allegedly attempted suicide in a Boston hotel on November 5, 1848, after scoring two ounces of laudanum. The author miscalculated the strength of the opiate and his overdose resulted in extreme sickness and a drug-induced delirium. After pulling himself together, he returned to Providence one last time to beg Whitman to marry him. She refused.

Based on several first-person accounts, Poe's spirit still haunts the steps outside the Providence Athenaeum and his ghost has been spotted near Whitman's house on Benefit Street. "People who have witnessed the specter state that he looks quite melancholy and when they attempt to address him, he either walks away quickly or vanishes," reported Thomas D'Agostino in *Ghosts of the Blackstone Valley*.

"Poe's connection with Providence, although brief, had a severe impact on the last years of his mortal life," D'Agostino told me. "Powerful emotions on both sides of the spectrum, love and broken love, may have been the catalysts that keep Poe's spirit roaming the rooms within the Athenaeum. His ghost is also seen walking down Benefit Street, stopping at the front door of Whitman's former home. Perhaps he's eternally trying to mend the broken relationship with her, or maybe it harkens back to a time when he was happily courting her. No one knows for sure because he never speaks."

Ocker, a skeptic when it comes to ghosts, said it's possible that there's a residual haunting of some sorts at the library where Poe courted his last love. "He definitely had feelings for her, even if part of it was because of economic reasons," Ocker explained. "He didn't want to be alone."

It was this tortured existence that has idolatrized the author, Ocker believes. "Considering all of the places that he lived, he never really belonged," he told me. "One of the reasons that Poe's legacy has survived is because he's universal. Poe was really not of this place."

Ocker said he's still trying to figure out Poe's indelible impact on pop culture. "The key to figuring out his popularity, which I haven't done yet, is how much of our media focuses directly on

Poe himself," Ocker explained. "We have this famous author and we adapt his works over and over again. Every time his work is adapted, we always seem to stick Poe in as a character."

It's the raven-haunted Poe that society seems to be obsessed with, Ocker said. "Without that, he probably wouldn't be a cult figure. If you look at the facts, he had a pretty rough life. At one point he turned down a party invitation because he had holes in his shoes."

Ultimately, there's a Poe-style twist that emerged posthumously. "The cosmic joke of it all is that

Boston-born author Edgar Allan Poe was honored with a commemorative statue on the corner of Boylston Street across from the Boston Common. PHOTO BY SAM BALTRUSIS.

after he dies, he becomes one of the most popular authors in the world," Ocker continued. "We love the underdog, but maybe there's something even more profound. There's hope in his story that we, like Poe, can somehow achieve greatness even after we die."

EDGAR ALLAN POE

Edgar Allan Poe had a love-hate relationship with his hometown. The author, who supposedly didn't like Boston, was born in the Bay Village but died in Baltimore at age forty in October 1849. In the late 1980s a local enthusiast was dead set on marking the spot where "The Raven" poet got his start. Norman George, a Poe performance artist, decided to create a plaque to commemorate the gothic writer's 180th birthday. The bronze tablet, made by Robert Shure from Woburn, was bolted to the building now occupied by the not-so-scary burrito joint Boloco, called "Poe-loco" by the locals, on the corner of Boylston Street and Charles Street South across from Boston Common.

In a *People* magazine story that chronicled the unveiling in 1989, the article referred to Poe as "Boston's least favorite son."

George, who recently passed, spilled to J.W. Ocker in *Poe-Land* that he wanted to honor his hometown hero. "When I was fourteen, my father took me down to Boston for a Boston University football game," George told Ocker. "While we were there, we looked for Poe's birthplace but just couldn't find it."

Poe tragically died in Baltimore, and the city seems to have claimed him as their own. Meanwhile, Boston has only recently embraced their "Poe-ness," unveiling a memorial statue in October 2014, around the corner from his birthplace. The square has become a major attraction honoring the mastermind behind "The Raven" and "The Tell-Tale Heart."

Poe was born in Boston on January 19, 1809. The offspring of two actors, the young Poe was sent to Virginia after his mother died and his father abandoned him.

He returned to the city of his birth in 1827 under financial duress. By the age of eighteen, Poe had amassed a considerable gambling debt. To raise funds and avoid his debt collectors, he joined the army under the fake name "Edgar A. Perry." Because he was too young to enlist, Poe lied and said he was twenty-two years old. Much to his chagrin, the soon-to-be-author's regiment was stationed at Fort Independence on South Boston's Castle Island.

While he reportedly wasn't happy with the homecoming, the Boston Harbor fort may have been inspiration for one of Poe's most popular stories, according to Peter Muise, author of *Legends and Lore of the North Shore.*

"One day Poe noticed a gravestone in the fort's cemetery for a Lt. Robert Massie, who had died on December 25, 1817," Muise recalled. "After Poe commented on the misfortune of dying on a holiday, one of his fellow soldiers told him the tragic story behind Massie's death."

Massie was well-liked by his peers at Fort Independence. However, one of his fellow officers, Gustavus Drane, had it in for the new recruit. Drane, an expert swordsman, argued with Massie over a card game on Christmas Eve and challenged him to a duel, killing Massie on December 25, 1817. Yes, it was Christmas day.

"The enlisted men were outraged, and as they dug Massie's grave they quietly plotted how to avenge his death," continued Muise. "A few nights after the duel they put their plan into action. First, they invited Drane to come drink with them. Once he was heavily inebriated they led him to an unused alcove inside the fort and chained him inside. Finally they walled up the alcove with bricks, sealing Drane inside forever."

According to lore, Poe was inspired by this real-life gruesome tale of revenge and the story was believed to be the basis for his 1846 classic "The Cask of Amontillado," where a man takes revenge on his drunken friend over an insult and ultimately entombs him alive.

Ocker, however, said it's highly unlikely that the poet drew inspiration from the story. "He was stationed on Castle Island and did enlist using a pseudonym in 1827. So, that part is true," Ocker told me. "He got his start on Castle Island and published fifty copies of his first volume of poetry, *Tamerlane,* using a 'by a Bostonian' byline, but was he inspired to write "The Cask of the Amontillado" while serving on Castle Island? Probably not."

In fact, there is even some debate about what really happened between Massie and Drane. "It does appear that Massie was actually killed by

Drane," said Muise, "but his killer was not entombed alive. Instead Drane avoided a court martial, moved to Philadelphia, and got married. He died in 1846 at the age of fifty-seven." Massie's remains were moved from Boston and reburied in Fort Devens.

While we may never know for sure what Poe's inspiration for that story was, historians believe that Il Buco, an Italian restaurant in Manhattan, may have also piqued Poe's interest. The Bond Street eatery has a cavernous cellar that was frequented by the poet. The area was part of the city's red-light district and the basement served as a saloon where alcohol, absinthe, and opium were served. Poe frequented the lower-level bar and exchanged letters with a young woman living on the third floor. Did Il Buco's basement inspire any of Poe's writing in 1846? It's possible. Poe's spirit supposedly haunts the underground space and employees claim to have seen the trailblazer's apparition emptying bottles. If the nineteenth-century cellar dweller is still hanging out, perhaps his ghost can confirm the rumors? Nevermore.

A crew of Brown University archaeologists did find the remains of two charred human skeletons in the early 1900s. Also, folklorist Edward Rowe Snow claimed that a skeleton wearing a military uniform buried in the bowels of Fort Independence was found in 1905. In *The Islands of Boston Harbor*, Snow wrote that Castle Island was cursed. According to pre-Revolutionary War legend, an English gentleman lived on the island with his daughter. The daughter had two suitors: One was British and had been picked by her father and the other was a colonist. She was smitten with the American boy, and the British man, enraged, challenged his competition to a duel. The Brit won, killing the young local. In a true *Romeo and Juliet* twist, the girl is said to have committed suicide in response to her beloved's death. "The British officer, heartbroken, rushed down to the dock and plunged into the channel, crying he would put a curse on all who ever came near the island," wrote Snow. "Some sailors still believe that many shipwrecks near the Castle are to be blamed on this curse."

Snow said Castle Island was known for its bizarre suicides, including a man who jumped to his death in 1903 and a Somerville man who shot himself in the head in one of Fort Independence's casemates.

Castle Island is also known for its sea serpent sightings. "They were seen in 1819, 1839, and 1931," added Muise. "There were a lot of sea serpent sightings off the North Shore, particularly in the nineteenth century, but sadly only a few have been seen in the harbor. Maybe it was just too busy or too polluted to sustain giant sea monsters?"

POE'S HAUNT: GARDNER-PINGREE MANSION

SALEM, MA— It's arguably Salem's crime of the century. The murder of Captain Joseph White, an eighty-two-year-old shipmaster and slave trader, riveted the nation in 1830 and inspired literary giants like Edgar Allan Poe and Nathaniel Hawthorne.

The crime scene, a three-story brick mansion built in 1804 and located at 128 Essex Street, is believed to boast a residual haunting, a psychic imprint of sorts, replaying the savage murder of White, who was whacked over the head with a twenty-two-inch piece of refurbished hickory, also known as an "Indian club," and stabbed thirteen times near his heart. According to several reports, a full-bodied apparition peeks out of the second-floor window. A female spirit rumored to be White's niece, Mary Beckford, who served as his housekeeper in addition to being his next of kin, is also said to haunt the Essex Street house. Beckford's daughter, also named Mary, was formerly part of the household in the 1820s, but moved to Wenham with her husband, Joseph Jenkins Knapp, Jr.

As far as the murder, it's a complicated puzzle that has been twisted over the years. Captain White's grand-nephew, Joe Knapp, learned that the retired merchant had just completed his will, leaving $15,000 to Mrs. Beckford. Knapp believed if White died without a will, his mother-in-law would inherit half his fortune of $200,000. So, Knapp and his brother John hired a black sheep from the respected Crowninshield family, Richard, to slay the captain in his sleep for a mere $1,000. Knapp had access to White's Essex Street home, and in April 1830, he stole the will and left the back parlor window unlocked. Beckford and her daughter Mary were staying in Wenham.

Richard Crowninshield slipped into the mansion at night "entering the house, stealthily threaded the staircase, softly opened the chamber door of the sleeping old man." He killed him with a single blow to the left temple, according to an account in the April 1830 edition of the *Salem Observer*. Crowninshield hid the murder weapons under the steps at the former Howard Street meetinghouse. The bludgeon, a hickory-stick club, was "fashioned to inflict a deadly blow with the least danger of breaking the skin. The handle was contrived as to yield a firm grasp to the hand."

As far as the crime scene, White was in his bedchamber lying diagonally across the bed on his right side. Blood strangely didn't ooze from the thirteen stab wounds because he died from the bludgeon and no valuables in the house were missing. Because there was no theft, police detectives were baffled at first. The Knapp brothers falsely claimed they had been robbed by three men en route to Wenham, which added some initial confusion to the murder mystery.

A gang of assassins in Salem? Yes, there were three, but it was the Knapp brothers and murder-for-hire crony Richard Crowninshield, who later hanged himself with a handkerchief tied to the bars of his prison cell before he was convicted. The Knapp brothers were then put on trial.

Daniel Webster, giving arguably one of his most famous legal orations, served as the Knapps' prosecutor and called the affair "a most extraordinary case" and a "cool, calculating, money making murder." The Knapp brothers, admitting they had planned the crime and fabricated the robbery story, were convicted. Meanwhile, it's believed that Edgar Allan Poe was inspired by Webster's speech and penned "The Tell-Tale Heart," a classic short story involving the guilt and retribution associated with the grisly murder of an older man. Hawthorne was also entranced by the trial and explored similar themes in *The Scarlet Letter* and *The House of the Seven Gables*.

Thousands gathered in downtown Salem to watch the public executions. John Francis Knapp was hanged on September 28, 1830, in front of a blood-soaked haunt from Salem's past: the former Witch Gaol, or witch dungeon, currently located at 10 Federal Street. His brother Joe, considered to be the mastermind behind the crime, met a similar fate three months later in November. The infamous murder weapon, the custom-made "Indian club" that measures more than twenty-two inches, is owned by the Peabody Essex Museum. Unfortunately, the macabre artifact isn't on display today, but visitors can tour the refurbished mansion.

Every major city has one: a murder house. Salem's is the Gardner-Pingree House. And, yes, it's supposedly haunted.

"There were two guys from Oregon who came here to debunk things and they captured on video what seems to be a man looking out of the window," recalled Tim Maguire from the Salem Night Tour. "Of all of the places we visit, we get the most photographic evidence from the Gardner-Pingree House. I've been inside the house a few times and I feel more of a presence of a woman. There's definitely a female presence there."

During a Graveyard Getaways tour I organized for a small group of investigators and paranormal enthusiasts, our crew was able to go inside the Gardner-Pingree House after visiting nearby Howard Street Cemetery. The consensus, which aligned with Maguire's observation, was that the structure had an intense, inexplicable energy.

"When I walked into that house it felt like a very inviting home," explained investigator Nicole Hellested. "As the tour continued, I started to feel like I was being watched. When we made our way up to the second floor I was overwhelmed with heaviness. I felt uneasy when I walked into the bedroom where the murder took place. I stepped in and then immediately out. I had a feeling that I shouldn't be in there and I needed to get out."

When asked if she believed that the Gardner-Pingree mansion is haunted, Hellested said yes without hesitation. "The house has a horrifying history and I think the spirits there want to keep it safe and protected," she added.

Russ Stiver, a veteran investigator and a sensitive to the paranormal, agreed with Hellested. "I almost had to leave the location because of the overwhelming energy present," he said. "It wasn't negative by any means, but very strong and protective over the house."

Stiver said he experienced a fight-or-flight reaction as the group inched toward the scene of the crime. "I didn't start to get anxious until I went to the second floor and toward the bedroom," he recalled. "I felt dizzy, sick to my stomach, and disoriented."

Brian Gerraughty, a skeptic among the group of investigators and sensitives, said he even felt strange on the second floor of the Gardner-Pingree House. "I didn't feel any negative energy entering the house or on the first floor at all, but there was an innate sense of foreboding going up to the second floor and especially entering the bedroom," he told me. "But I'm not a sensitive in any true respect."

Psychic imprint from the past? Paranormal investigators such as Adam Berry from *Kindred Spirits* believe that residual energy associated with heinous crimes, specifically murders, has potential to leave a supernatural imprint. "Anytime there's a traumatic event, it could be left behind," Berry said. "If you walk into a room and two people have been arguing, fiercely, you can feel that weirdness that they've created or energy they emit spewing at each other. I do think there's a form of energy that can be left behind from a traumatic event or any kind of murder or suicide in a room. The theory is that maybe that energy goes into the walls and lingers there."

According to several reports, the historic murder repeats itself spectrally on the anniversary of Captain White's death. There are also many sightings of a male phantom, believed to be White or possibly one of the Knapp brothers or even Richard Crowninshield, gazing out of the second floor of the Gardner-Pingree House as the living frolic up and down Essex Street. If the mansion's male spirit truly has a calendar, his next scheduled appearance is April 6.

As for the city's penchant for historical coincidences, the family home of White's murderer, the Crowninshield-Bentley House, was literally moved next to the crime scene in 1959. Yep, the murderer's house was placed next-door to the murder house. Sometimes fact is stranger than fiction.

EUGENE O'NEILL

Playwright Eugene O'Neill apparently had some unfinished business when he died tragically on November 27, 1953, in Room 401 of the former Sheraton Hotel, now Kilachand Hall, a Boston University–owned dormitory.

Son of Irish immigrant actor James O'Neill and Mary Ellen Quinlan, *The Iceman Cometh* author suffered severe Parkinson's-like tremors caused by the late onset of a genetic neurological disease called cerebellar cortical atrophy, which he suffered from in his fifties until his death at age sixty-five. O'Neill was also a notorious alcoholic. As his health deteriorated, he insisted that he "wanted no priest or minister, or Salvation Army captain at his deathbed." He continued, "I will face God, if there is a God, face to face, man to man." The uncontrollable shaking impaired his ability to write, and he struggled with tremors later in life, allegedly asking his wife Carlotta to destroy many of his uncompleted plays.

For the record, Carlotta initially claimed that she and her husband burned the unfinished manuscripts in a fireplace in the hotel, but there are no fireplaces in the building. After questioning from reporters, Carlotta later recanted the story, saying she destroyed the unfinished plays, shredding the pages and then handing them to a janitor who burned the shreds in an incinerator located in the building's basement.

These so-called phantom conversations may have inspired Carlotta to release O'Neill's autobiographical masterpiece, *Long Day's Journey Into Night*, in 1956 even though he had clearly stipulated that he didn't want to make it public until twenty-five years after his death. Perhaps O'Neill's postmortem spirit had a change of heart. He posthumously won the Pulitzer Prize in 1957.

The former hotel turned college dormitory where he died is reportedly haunted. "Strange things do happen," said former Kilachand Hall resident Stephanie Lui to *BU Today* in 2009. "For example, there was a period of time at night when a gust of wind would blow underneath the door from the hallway into our room. It made a loud noise, and we couldn't figure out why wind would be blowing within the building."

David Zamojski, assistant dean of students and director of residence life at BU, insisted that some still believe the urban legend. "Students have been telling stories about O'Neill's spirit and ghost as long as I've been here," he said. "We have received reports of many strange incidents."

Zamojski, in an interview with the *Daily Free Press*, mentioned phenomenon like flickering lights and phantom knocks. "I remember hearing stories from students that they would hear sounds, like doors closing or knocks at the door. When they opened their own doors, there would be no one out in the corridor," he said. "I even remember a student saying that she had seen sort of a shadowy figure in the corridor."

Of course Kilachand Hall isn't the only haunted location with ties to the playwright. The O'Neill Center in New London, Connecticut, is reportedly teeming with ghosts from his past. Monte Cristo Cottage, which served as inspiration for two of O'Neill's plays—*Ah, Wilderness!* and *Long Day's Journey Into Night*—was his childhood summer home. Visitors have reported phantom footsteps and "cold spots," a sign of paranormal activity, since the center acquired the property in the 1970s.

Railroad tycoon Edward Crowninshield Hammond, known to shoo O'Neill from his private property facing Waterford Beach, was vilified as an out-of-touch millionaire named Harker in *Long Day's Journey into Night*. In a serendipitous twist of fate, the O'Neill Center acquired Hammond's aged mansion in 1964 and turned it into the home for the Playwrights Conference.

According to *Theater Mania*'s Michael Feingold, the plutocrat's former home was extremely haunted when a motley crew of theater types first set up shop. "At least two ghosts were rumored to stalk its corridors, one of them the spirit of old Mrs. Hammond, who had been a leader in the social ostracism of Ella O'Neill, and whose postmortem reaction to finding her earthly domicile occupied by a crowd of raffish theater people was emphatically negative. Many eerie occurrences were reported," wrote Feingold in "Notes on O'Neill's Ghosts" in June 2016. "Playwrights were warned not to doze off in the third-floor library, a comfortable retreat that had quickly become their workroom and hangout," Feingold continued. "Some who did do so reported being awakened by a hard shove, or a sudden chill, to find a disembodied pair of red eyes glaring at them."

While the "otherworldly manifestations of disapproval" have simmered down at the Monte Cristo Cottage and Hammond mansion in Connecticut, the ghostly reports from the Writers' Corridor at Kilachand Hall continue. Yes, all the world's a stage . . . and all of the lingering spirits are merely players.

O'NEILL'S HAUNT: ATLANTIC HOUSE

PROVINCETOWN, MA— Built in 1798 by Provincetown's first postmaster, Daniel Pease, the Atlantic House was the last stagecoach stop until 1873 for commuters coming in from Orleans. Known as the Union House in the 1800s, it was also a regular watering hole for America's more infamous turn-of-the-century writers, including Eugene O'Neill and Tennessee Williams. According to several accounts, the now off-limits quarters upstairs at the A-House are a hot spot for paranormal activity.

"The A-House is definitely haunted," confirmed Ashley Shakespeare, a veteran ghost tour guide and regular performer in Provincetown. "There are residual haunts especially in the guest house. When I was in the cast of the show *Painted Ladies*, our dressing room was upstairs in the old guest house. Lights would turn on and doors would open and close."

Shakespeare, who is sensitive to the paranormal, said the activity at the Atlantic House isn't intelligent. The energy, he explained, is residual— or like a videotaped replay of past events. "I feel the A-House is most haunted with residual energy, from back when Judy Garland, Billie Holiday, Eartha Kitt, and so many other greats were entertaining there," he claimed. "I have been in the A-House during the day by myself and could feel this great energy and presence."

The excitement of past performers, he said, has left a psychic imprint on the historic structure. "It was almost as if a live band was coming up through the floor and an audience just started to appear buzzing about whichever great performer was about to appear," the drag illusionist continued. "It was magical."

Of course, the building's well-known former tenant, playwright Eugene O'Neill, could have left an indelible mark on the allegedly haunted guest house.

"In the late spring of 1917, O'Neill and his friend Harold DePolo, a pulp fiction writer and proficient drinking partner, were arrested on charges of espionage at the still-operating Atlantic House bar in Provincetown," explained Robert M. Dowling in his book, *Critical Companion to Eugene O'Neill.* "Secret Service agents were summoned from Boston, as the United States had just entered the First World War and there was a general scare of German spies on American soil. The bohemian vagabonds looked highly suspicious to local Provincetowners—particularly O'Neill, who was carrying a black satchel that appeared as if it might contain surveillance equipment but was most likely his typewriter case."

O'Neill spent the night in the basement of Provincetown's town hall, which is also reportedly haunted, but was released when he was identified as the son of his famous father, actor James O'Neill.

Mary Heaton Vorse, author of *Time and the Town: A Provincetown Chronicle*, said that O'Neill was the subject of a full-blown witch hunt. "The poor man was persecuted," Vorse wrote. "There was talk of running him out town, of arresting him, when Max Bohm, the famous painter, came furiously to his assistance and shamed the witch-hunters into silence and sanity."

If O'Neill is, in fact, haunting the Atlantic House, he's double dipping in the afterlife.

Students at Kilachand Hall in Boston, formerly Shelton Hall, claim the playwright haunts the dorm's Writers' Corridor on the fourth floor. The *Long Day's Journey Into Night* author—crippled with a slew of ailments ranging from a rare genetic neurological disease to tuberculosis to depression to stomach disorders exacerbated by alcoholism—spent the last two years of his life in suite 401, when the BU dormitory, located at 91 Bay State Road, was a Sheraton-owned hotel. Kilachand was originally built in 1923. In a strange twist of fate, O'Neill was born in a hotel, the Barrett, located at 1500 Broadway in the heart of New York City's Times Square.

O'Neill spent his last days downing shots of whiskey in suite 401 to numb both his emotional and physical pain. He forced the liquor down his throat and, in essence, drank himself to death. His famous last words? "Born in a hotel room and goddammit, died in a hotel room," he reportedly whispered to his wife Carlotta three days before his final curtain call in 1953.

Carlotta, who moved into the building in 1951 because of its proximity to her shrink's office on Bay State Road, insisted that her husband's ghost was in the room and that he talked to her into the wee hours of the night.

Boston University purchased the Bay State Road structure in 1954, and Carlotta soon checked out. However, her famous husband's tortured soul is rumored to remain in Kilachand Hall. Reports of the elevator mysteriously stopping on the fourth floor, phantom knocks, unexplained gusts of wind, and inexplicably dim lights continue to creep out students who live there.

Oddly, the hauntings reported at the A-House's upstairs guest house echo the types of phenomenon at the Boston University dorm, including phantom knocking, inexplicable cold spots, and doors opening and closing.

Is O'Neill taking a post-mortem vacation at his former haunt in Provincetown? Apparently, the show must go on—even in the afterlife.

HARRIET BEECHER STOWE

When it comes to Victorian-era spirit board communication, Harriet Beecher Stowe was in the know. In fact, she wrote about her exploits in personal letters and even tried to reach out to one of the Brontë sisters.

"Like many nineteenth-century Americans, she had an open mind about connecting with those who were no longer living," reads the website for the Harriet Beecher Stowe Center. "Stowe's interest in Spiritualism, the belief that spirits of the dead can and do communicate with the living, helped ease the pain of losing four of seven children during her lifetime."

Stowe even explored ghostly themes in her work. According to the center's website, "The paranormal occasionally showed up in her writing as well; she included a ghost story in *Uncle Tom's Cabin*, her most famous work written in 1852."

In Stowe's seminal saga, she hinted at the paranormal when Tom visited Legree plantation. In the chapter called "An Authentic Ghost Story," Legree slowly goes mad when he hears strange noises coming from the garret. Convinced that the phantom sounds are ghostly manifestations, he uses alcohol to self-medicate, which leads to his demise. Cassy, the man's enslaved sex worker, puts on a shroud worn by the plantation owner's dead mother and, during one of her nightly visits, terrifies the man to a point of mentally pushing him over the edge. With Legree on his deathbed, Cassy and Emmeline escape from the horrors of the plantation.

The *Uncle Tom's Cabin* author also experimented with the spirit board, a precursor to the modern-day Ouija, which was discussed in a personal correspondence sent to her overseas pen pal, George Eliot. Eliot was really Stowe's friend and *Middlemarch* author Mary Anne Evans, who used "George Eliot" as her *nom de plume*.

In a letter dated May 11, 1872, Stowe openly talked about her spirit board communication with Charlotte Brontë, author of *Jane Eyre*. She discussed using her "toy planchette" to chat with the eldest Brontë sister who passed on March 31, 1855. In the session, the ghost seemed to be rolling in her grave because critics called her work "coarse." Stowe was curious if Brontë was upset about the criticisms when she was alive. For the record, she definitely was irked.

Unfortunately, we don't have Eliot's response. But we do know that Stowe believed she was communicating with a spirit, but not completely convinced it was actually Brontë. "Spirits unseen have communicated with me I cannot doubt," she wrote.

In one point during the letter, Stowe suggested that another entity was posing as the *Jane Eyre* author. Then she recanted her previous comment by writing, "I must hope much in this hereafter Charlotte speaks of."

Was it Brontë's ghost? Perhaps. Did Stowe believe in spirits? Yes.

During her heyday, Stowe was the most revered writer in the States and abroad. A die-hard abolitionist, she was a rebel with a cause. President Abraham Lincoln famously called her "the little lady that made this big war," referring to the spark known as *Uncle Tom's Cabin* that ignited the Civil War. And while she was arguably best known for *Uncle Tom's Cabin*, Stowe wrote hundreds of novels, short stories, articles, and children's books. She also penned a spooky tale called "A Ghost in the Mill." Set in Boston, the story follows Captain Eb Sawin who ends up at Cack Sparrock's creepy old mill during a snowstorm. The moral of the eerie tale is no matter how far you run from something, it will always catch up to you. And, yes, her ghosts usually had an anti-slavery subtext.

Using the spirit realm as a literary device, Stowe protested the norms of the day, specifically slavery. In her subtle-but-visionary take on the genre, the writer's apparitions seek postmortem justice. In fact, her fearsome phantoms were protesting the societal norms that ultimately killed them when they were alive. Yes, good triumphs over evil . . . even in the afterlife.

STOWE'S HAUNT: BEECHER STOWE CENTER

HARTFORD, CT—There's a weird, inexplicable energy that lingers around Harriet Beecher Stowe's Gothic-style home adjacent to the equally creepy Mark Twain House at 77 Forest Street in Hartford, Connecticut. The Civil War–era author lived here for twenty-three years until she passed on July 1, 1896. According to my tour guide, Rodrigo Pinto, the reports of ghostly activity in the house museum include blinds mysteriously opening and closing and the sound of phantom footsteps coming from upstairs when there is no one on the second floor.

Pinto, who regularly gives history tours in the house during the day, said that while he has never had a paranormal experience personally, he's heard of a "lingering energy associated with Harriet reaching out to her lost sons, including Harry and the son [Fredrick William] who died mysteriously after fighting in the Civil War."

"Folks say in the parlor, window shades open on their own and all over the building footsteps have been heard," according to HauntedPlaces.com. "Flashes of light have been seen in the bedrooms, and an apparition was seen in the visitor's center."

Amanda Roy, a former program coordinator at the center, was interviewed by *CTNow*, a weekly newspaper published by *the Hartford Courant*, in a video called *Haunted History*. In the segment, Roy alluded to Stowe's belief in the afterlife. "We don't have records of Stowe practicing séances in this house, but we do know that she did attend séances because she had so much loss in her life," Roy said, adding that "there have been a few instances, when the house was open for public tours, footsteps were heard going up the stairs."

The tremendous loss in Stowe's life involved several of her children. In 1851, her eighteen-month-old son Samuel Charles died from cholera. Historians say the infant's death helped her empathize with the experience of an enslaved mother losing her child, which was the central storyline in *Uncle Tom's Cabin*. Stowe lost her eldest son, Henry Ellis, in a freak swimming accident in the Connecticut River while he attended Dartmouth College in 1857. He was only nineteen. Her fourth child, Frederick William, struggled with addiction issues and was discharged from the army because of his alcoholism. He died on his way to San Francisco, California, in 1871.

Stowe's husband Calvin was also a big believer in spirits, which may have had an impact on his wife. "Calvin Stowe felt a connection with the spirits when he was a child and that lasted all the way up until adulthood," Roy explained. "He even saw an apparition of his [first] wife, Eliza Tyler Stowe, who passed away before he married Harriet."

The Harriet Beecher Stowe cottage has been investigated by local groups, including CT Old School Paranormal. Dan Rivera, from the Connecticut-based team of investigators, said that he's had inexplicable experiences in the gray, two-story home, which was built in 1871. "I believe there's activity going on inside the house. I want to say that there's an intelligent haunting in there," Rivera told *CTNow*.

Margaurite Carter, also from CT Old School Paranormal, said that the team picked up an eerie electronic voice phenomenon (EVP) in the house that clearly said, "Read my journal." Another member from the team claimed to have seen a full-bodied apparition of a woman wearing a burgundy-colored dress. When the investigator approached the spirit, it mysteriously disappeared.

Roy said she believes there's a lingering, benevolent energy still hanging out in the Harriet Beecher Stowe Center. "This is not a spooky house where people will jump out at you or anything like that," Roy said in the *Haunted History* video. "Whether you believe in ghosts or not, the lives of the people who used to live here are still sticking around."

H.P. LOVECRAFT

Howard Phillips Lovecraft created some of the freakiest monsters unleashed in the dark recesses of our imagination. He's the mad genius behind "The Call of Cthulhu," which featured an aquatic creature lurking in a post-apocalyptic state of slumber at the bottom of the ocean. His army of ancient beings from the Cthulhu Mythos—featured in stories such as "The Rats in the Walls," "At the Mountains of Madness," and "The Shadow Over Innsmouth"—terrorized pulp fiction fanatics.

While there's no doubt that H.P. Lovecraft was sick and twisted on paper, don't judge a man by his make-believe monsters. In reality he was a poverty-stricken visionary tormented by extreme loss, involuntary tics, and nervous breakdowns. While his Lovecraftian creations were visceral and unabashedly disturbing, it was his personal demons and odd quirks that catapulted him into the upper echelon of horror writers. Yes, life imitates art. Like many of the authors featured in this book, he didn't become famous until after his death on March 15, 1937. He was only forty-six years old.

J.W. Ocker, author of *Poe-Land*, said that Lovecraft's tragic life as a struggling artist oddly echoed Edgar Allan Poe's sad-sack journey. "Lovecraft followed an arc similar to Poe," Ocker told me. "The embracing of Lovecraft has just started. For Poe, it was fifty years until he had a proper gravestone."

In comparison to Boston's lackluster response to Poe, Ocker said that Rhode Island's capital has honored its horror icon. "I've been going to Providence for ten years. Nowadays, there are several monuments to him and there's a rise in Lovecraft's popularity," he explained. "The Internet and Cthulhu have helped him out a lot. We all know the monster with tentacles."

There was a backlash over Lovecraft's xenophobic point of view that could be categorized as racist. Ocker said that Lovecraft, like Poe, was probably a product of his times. "There's a backlash against him because of his beliefs," Ocker said. "He was turned into a figure instead of person with real beliefs and problems."

Lovecraft was born on August 20, 1890. His father, Winfield, was hospitalized in 1893 after a psychotic episode that was likely fueled by untreated syphilis and ultimately led to his death in 1898. Lovecraft grew up in his family home in Providence and lived with his mother, Susie, as well as his maternal aunts and grandparents, Whipple and Robie. After his father's hospitalization, Lovecraft was enamored with his grandfather Whipple's dispatches of the strange and macabre that he relayed to his grandson during business trips abroad. Lovecraft was also close to his grandmother Robie and he was devastated when she passed in 1896.

As a child, Lovecraft was tortured by night terrors and recurring dreams he termed as "nightgaunts." He was also afraid of the dark. In 1904 his beloved grandfather died from a stroke after losing the family fortune. Scarred by death and financial despair, Lovecraft had severe insomnia-driven episodes and had a full-blown nervous breakdown during high school. His plan was to attend Brown University but he dropped out of school completely and never earned a college degree.

It was during this period that Lovecraft developed an affinity for astronomy and would spend days at the Ladd Observatory in Providence. "As a child, his family was good friends with Winslow Upton, director of the observatory and he was given a key to come and go as he pleased. He found much contentment there and often visited the building. It's no doubt that many of his stories and characters were born in that edifice while he gazed out into the abyss of the heavens," Thomas D'Agostino, author of *Haunted Rhode Island*, told me.

He also went on to claim that, "Lovecraft is said to haunt the observatory." According to D'Agostino, the author's spirit has been spotted by visitors who frequent Brown University's astronomical observatory located at 210 Doyle Avenue. "People claim to have seen his ghost peering out the window of the observatory or wandering the grounds in front of the building," he explained. "People also get a strange feeling like they are not alone while in the observatory."

Like Poe, Lovecraft's ghost has also been seen at the Providence Athenaeum. In fact, D'Agostino believes that "his presence is alive in many places along the East Side where he lived and died."

Lovecraft married Sonia Greene on March 3, 1924, and the two lived in the Red Hook neighborhood of Brooklyn, New York. Struggling to make a living writing stories for *Weird Tales* magazine, Lovecraft returned to Providence and eventually had an amicable breakup with Greene. In early 1937, he was diagnosed with cancer of the small intestines and passed in March.

The horror writer is listed along with his parents on the Phillips family monument in Swan Point Cemetery on Blackstone Road. In 1977, fans of the author erected a commemorative headstone in the burial ground with the famous line pulled from his letters declaring, "I am Providence." Apparently, Rhode Island's capital city agrees with Lovecraft.

LOVECRAFT'S HAUNT: PROVIDENCE BILTMORE

PROVIDENCE, RI—The Providence Biltmore (now called the Graduate Providence) opened on June 6, 1922, and boasts an almost too-good-to-be-true past that rivals some of pop culture's more infamous hotels. In fact, it's often said to be the inspiration for the Overlook in Stephen King's *The Shining* and the Bates Motel in *Psycho*. True? Probably not.

However, the Biltmore does host a Lovecraft-inspired convention. The biennial NecronomiCon celebrates weird fiction and academia in H.P. Lovecraft's hometown. Of course, the festival is held in one of New England's most haunted locations. A hotel where guests check in but don't check out? Yes, the Providence Biltmore has that notorious reputation.

The Beaux-Arts-style building located at 11 Dorrance Street in downtown Providence was designed by Warren and Wetmore, who also built Grand Central Terminal in Manhattan. The hotel was a Sheraton-owned structure for years, and it was flooded in 1954 after Hurricane Carol decimated the Ocean State. In fact, there's a plaque in the lobby demarcating the flood waters, which reached almost eight feet during the storm.

Named "America's Most Haunted Hotel" in 2000 by the American Hotel & Lodging Association, the Providence Biltmore was allegedly financed by practicing Satanist Johan Leisse Weisskopf, who supposedly wanted to showcase his religion to New England's not-so-puritanical denizens. The original design included a poultry farm on the roof with a working chicken coop. According to a far-fetched legend, the fowl were sacrificed in a blood ritual, and the basement was used for purification ceremonies.

The second floor was home to the scantily-clad Bacchante Girls, who paraded around the Garden Room and served luminaries such as Douglas Fairbanks, F. Scott and Zelda Fitzgerald, and Louis Armstrong. Because of its naughty reputation and Weisskopf's ties to the Rhode Island mafia, the Providence Biltmore became a hotbed of nefarious activity during the Prohibition era, and a series of murders and sexual assaults are said to have occurred at the grand hotel from 1920 to 1933, including a horrific drowning involving an eleven-year-old prostitute in one of the room's bathtubs.

"Among the hauntings reported, the sound of raucous parties has been heard by guests for decades, as well as locked doors suddenly unlocking; the sound of laughter; and moving orbs, especially on the sixteenth floor; as well as the apparition of a female spirit," reported Robert A. Geake in *Historic Taverns of Rhode Island*. "In his book, *Haunted Providence*, mentalist Rory Raven also reported sightings of an unfortunate stockbroker who plunged to his death from the fourteenth floor on Black Tuesday in 1929. The room where he stayed is reportedly haunted, and guests are sometimes startled by the unsettling vision of a man falling past their windows to the street below."

When I booked my overnight stay at this notoriously haunted hotel, I intuitively knew it was going to be one hell of a night. In fact, I read that the Providence Biltmore has a reputation for guests going missing under mysterious circumstances. One reported case of people vanishing from the hotel was as recent as 2008. I sheepishly warned my friends to send out a search party if they didn't hear from me.

The lobby, which resembles Grand Central Terminal in New York City, oozed a "something wicked this way comes" vibe. Courtney, the spunky, front-desk concierge, said she technically hadn't had any first-hand encounters with ghosts at the hotel. However, she does often retell guests a story from her first day on the job at the historic haunt. "I was nervous about working at what was supposedly one of the most haunted hotels in New England," she told me. "During my first night at the hotel, I walked into one of the empty rooms with the lights out, and I saw what looked like a shadow figure reflected in the mirror. The dark mass was in the shape of a person. When I turned on the lights, I realized it was me. It was my reflection."

The concierge jokingly said she fabricated the story. However, I wasn't convinced it was totally made up. When Courtney recounted the tall tale, she had fear in her eyes.

My room was on the twelfth floor and was in the "drop zone" of the man who plunged to his death in 1929. According to reports, the residual energy haunts all the rooms he passes. As far as the residual haunting is concerned, it's almost like a videotaped replay of a traumatic event that occurred years ago.

On the second floor, outside of the former Bacchante Room, I met with demonologist James Annitto and his paranormal friend Russ Stiver. We were focused on the symbols scattered throughout the Providence Biltmore's ornate lobby, which featured a recurring sphinx motif and an urn. So many labyrinthine rooms and secret entrances surrounded us, we almost got lost in what seemed like a maze of haunted history. Both Annitto and Stiver felt a heavy presence on the mezzanine level.

After taking a trip to the top floor, which had a past life as a chicken coop, the twenty-seven-year-old demonologist and I talked about the rumored animal sacrifices that had occurred in the hotel. "Most blood rituals are bad news," Annitto told me. "During a blood sacrifice, you're requesting a spirit or entity to come forward. When people conjure some-thing, they think they can contain it . . . but they can't. The entity plays to the human's requests, but it's controlling your every step. The blood ritual creates a fundamental energy shift at a location, and it amplifies the haunting."

Stiver is an empath. He talked about the large number of unreported suicides and deaths he sensed had occurred at the hotel. "Sordid activities have left an imprint on the building," he said. "When you walk into this place, you immediately feel the heaviness."

During our discussion on the historic second floor, Stiver felt a spirit lurking over his shoulder. "I'm getting a middle-aged gentleman. The hotel was a playground for people, and he came here on business . . . but it was definitely for pleasure," Stiver said.

The demonologist agreed with the empath. "There is so much history in Providence and specifically at this hotel," Annitto said nervously, looking over Stiver's shoulder. "I'm in construction, and when you start building a hotel like the Providence Biltmore, deaths happen. I bet many people have died here and that includes all of the unreported deaths and suicides that have happened in this hotel over the past century."

I jokingly called the Providence Biltmore "suicide central," and when I glanced up, I saw what looked like a lady in white dart past the entrance to the second floor's State Room. I initially called her a "flapper ghost," but in hindsight she looked more like she was from the late 1930s or early 1940s. We quickly gathered our belongings and followed the spirit down several hallways that led us to a wall display of historical artifacts.

In one of the photos, showcased among other hotel ephemera, there seemed to be a group of sailors and women enjoying one last night together before the men headed overseas. The photo oddly reminded me of the final scene from *The Shining* when viewers realize that the film's contemporary antagonist, Jack Torrance, is somehow in the photo from a New Year's Eve bash at the Overlook Hotel in 1921.

I told Annitto and Stiver about a key I'd received in the mail, and I immediately received a spirit communication from the ghost lady in the hallway begging me to take a closer look at the photo. I looked again at the historic picture and saw a woman in white. She looked upset. She was sitting next to a sailor. Based on the room's decor in the picture, it was a celebration of sorts, possibly a dance.

Was the lady in white luring me to the hotel so she could tell me her story? In the wee hours of the night, after Annitto and Stiver had left, I returned to the State Room area where I'd encountered the lady in white. I walked down the long corridor with my EVP recorder in hand. My goal was to communicate with the spirit again and hopefully get some answers.

When I approached the hallway with the glass-encased photo, a security guard popped out of nowhere and politely told me that the area was off limits to guests. He locked the door, and I wasn't able to access the artifacts hidden in the hotel's corridor of secrets.

Last dance at the Providence Biltmore? I will probably never know for sure what happened to the lady in white. However, based on my sleepless night at this extremely haunted hotel in Providence, the hotel's Prohibition-era party continues in the afterlife.

GHOST ADVENTURE:
SHINING AT THE STANLEY

"I dreamed of my three-year-old son running through the corridors, looking back over his shoulder, eyes wide, screaming. He was being chased by a firehose."

—Stephen King, author of *The Shining*

Surrounded by props from the made-for-television miniseries based on Stephen King's *The Shining*, I'm sitting in a dark room located in the bowels of the haunted Stanley Hotel in Estes Park, Colorado. There's a Big Wheel bike that little Danny Torrance famously rides through the empty hallways of the fictional Overlook Hotel, an old-school typewriter with the "all work and no play" line typed over and over into reams of paper and a creepy movie still from Stanley Kubrick's horror classic featuring the murdered Grady girls who begged the tormented boy to come play with them.

The Stanley Hotel is a Colonial Revival–style hotel located in Estes Park, Colorado. PHOTO COURTESY DEPOSIT PHOTOS.

"Wendy, I'm home," I said to myself as my ghost tour guide, Olivia, flicked the lights on and off to get the group's attention.

"Are we excited for some spirit action tonight? I know it's late but bring that energy for the full seventy-five minutes because that's going to help you have your interactions tonight," Olivia announced to our small but enthusiastic group. "Our spirits can't go to Starbucks to get that motivation, alright? Keep an eye on your electronic devices because you may see them do some bizarre things. Yes, your battery levels may go up and down and your phone may take photos that you didn't necessarily intend to take. Most importantly, pay attention to your personal energy. If our spirits like you, they may borrow a piece of your energy."

Olivia's approach to the Stanley Hotel's ghost tour seemed oddly like a paranormal pep rally. I was waiting for the perky, twenty-something guide to start an impromptu, spirit-squad cheer. *We got spirits, yes we do. We got spirits, how 'bout you?*

"If you notice your energy drop, the spirits may be trying to connect with you. However, if you feel completely drained it may not be what you're thinking," she explained. "No, you're not being possessed. It's most likely elevation sickness. But if you do feel a possession coming on, let me know. I don't want anyone to pass out on my tour."

Despite the dark subject matter, Olivia's enthusiasm was infectious. An overnight stay at the Stanley Hotel had always been high on my bucket list. Finally, I was able to tour the hotel that inspired *The Shining.*

I was giddy with excitement. Or was it elevation sickness?

My first taste of horror master Stephen King was the movie version of *Carrie.* I remember identifying with the bullied protagonist who painfully dealt with a dirty little secret. While battling her religious zealot of a mother and the gum-smacking sadism of cruel teenagers, Carrie White unsuccessfully tried to control her burgeoning ability to move things with her mind. Like White, I didn't quite fit into the status quo of the 1970s. Unlike King's cursed anti-hero, I didn't have latent telekinetic powers.

But I did have a secret.

There was something about King's *The Shining* that tapped into my darkest childhood fears. I remember riding the school bus when I was younger and waiting for my friend to recount the eerie stories that unfolded in King's archetypal ghost story. I was so terrified that I wasn't able to actually read the book until junior high.

Why was I scared? Like young Danny in *The Shining*, I was dealing with the unnerving ability to detect spirits. I could also pick up on the lingering energy at haunted locations. At the time, I had no idea what was going on with me. What did the spirits from my childhood want from me? I didn't view the ability as a gift. It was a curse.

When Chef Dick Hallorann explained to the troubled Danny why the disembodied souls from the Overlook continued to linger, it helped me understand what I was experiencing as a kid who also had empathic abilities. "I don't know why, but it seems that all the bad things that ever happened here, there's little pieces of those things still laying around like fingernail clippings," Hallorann warned. Past traumatic events like murders and suicides could leave a psychic imprint on a building, according to the telepathic chef. "Some places are like people: Some shine, some don't," he said.

Much like its fictional counterpart in *The Shining*, the Stanley closed during the winters until 1983. When King and his wife Tabitha stayed at the hotel in late September 1974, the Estes Park hideaway was preparing for hibernation mode.

"We were the only guests as it turned out," King recalls on his website. "The following day they were going to close the place down for the winter. Wandering through its corridors, I thought that it seemed the perfect setting for a ghost story."

The horror writer was inspired by a dream he had while staying in the notoriously haunted Room 217. "That night I dreamed of my three-year-old son running through the corridors, looking back over his shoulder, eyes wide, screaming. He was being chased by a firehose," King continued. "I woke up with a tremendous jerk, sweating all over, within an inch of falling out of bed. I got up, lit a cigarette, sat in the chair looking out the window at the Rockies, and by the time the cigarette was done, I had the bones of the book firmly set in my mind."

Before flying out to the Rocky Mountain location that inspired King, I reached out to my fellow ghost writer and friend, Richard Estep. Originally from the United Kingdom, he's armed with more than twenty years of experience investigating the paranormal on both sides of the pond. Estep, currently based in the Denver area, is the author of several historical-based ghost books, including *Haunted Longmont* and *In Search of the Paranormal*. He's also a part-time tour guide at the Stanley Hotel.

"When I applied for a tour guide job at the Stanley three years ago, I was somewhat skeptical of the hauntings," Estep told me. "It didn't take long for me to learn firsthand that the hotel is genuinely paranormally active, and is a truly fascinating place to work and visit."

Why are locations like the Stanley more haunted than other structures? "Hotels see the entire spectrum of human life, good and bad, and that leaves an imprint of some kind that we cannot yet explain," Estep said.

Opened on July 4, 1909, the hotel was the brainchild of the Yankee steam-powered car inventor, Freelan Oscar Stanley. Suffering from pulmonary tuberculosis, F.O. Stanley spearheaded the forty-eight-room grand hotel as a health retreat for New England's upper crust seeking the curative air of the Rocky Mountains. Stanley's wife Flora relocated with her husband, and the duo spent their summers entertaining in Estes Park, Colorado. He sold the hotel in 1926 and purchased it again in 1929. In 1940 Stanley died from a heart attack in Newton, Massachusetts, one year after his wife passed.

Estep said that King and the Stanley are now inextricably intertwined in the public consciousness. "His influence is still felt at the hotel to this day, from the annual Shining Ball to the throngs of visitors who visit the Stanley because of its connection to King and *The Shining*," Estep explained. "Room 217 is the hotel's most popular room—and its most infamous—and generates a regular stream of seemingly inexplicable experiences."

Before my overnight stay at the Stanley, I had a spirit communication with a female ghost that appeared to be associated with the hotel. Based on an unnerving dream I had at my brother's house in nearby Highlands Ranch the night before my visit, I believe she was waiting for me. When I woke up, my ankles mysteriously started to hurt.

When I asked Estep about the spirit-induced dream, he said that I possibly connected with the hotel's former housekeeper, Elizabeth Wilson, who was injured in a freak accident in 1911. "Miss Wilson was a chambermaid caught in the gas explosion of Room 217," Estep told me. "She didn't die in the hotel, but was injured, and returned to the Stanley after her convalescence, where she spent many happy years working there."

Believe it or not, Wilson had broken both of her ankles during the blast.

The Stanley Hotel served as the inspiration for the Overlook Hotel in Stephen King's 1977 bestselling novel *The Shining*. PHOTO COURTESY DEPOSIT PHOTOS.

Estep said that the acetylene gas explosion—accidentally caused by Wilson when she walked into the suite with a lit candle—may have psychically imprinted itself on the Stanley. "I believe that she is still connected to the hotel after her death because she was so attached to the place during her physical lifetime," he said. "One disrespects her at their peril."

According to legend, Wilson worked at the Stanley until she passed in the 1950s. Her lingering spirit supposedly unpacks and folds the clothing of unsuspecting guests. She also has an issue with unmarried couples sleeping in the same bed. Wilson's ghost reportedly doesn't like what she sees as improper behavior in the hotel. In fact, the former chambermaid has forcibly tried to separate unwed couples by creeping in between them in the wee hours of the night.

When I checked into my room at the Stanley, I was somewhat relieved that I was assigned to Room 213. It's not haunted, right? When I mentioned to Olivia, my tour guide, that I was a few doors down from the infamous Room 217, she laughed. "All of the rooms in that wing were part of the presidential suite," she said. "So, Room 217—as well as 213, 215, and 219—had all been one giant suite."

It had happened again. I was put into a haunted room. Why was I not surprised?

Our first stop on the ghost tour was the Concert Hall. I had been warned by my author friend that the Stanley's music venue, originally an entertainment complex called The Casino, which also had a subterranean bowling alley, was teeming with ghostly activity. "Paranormally speaking, the Concert Hall is the most active part of the entire hotel," Estep had said.

During the tour of the Concert Hall, I saw what looked like a shadow figure dart by the stairwell next to the stage and I heard a female spirit say "open" when I headed down to the basement. According to Estep, I may have encountered the spirits of Paul, who died while shoveling snow outside of the performance space in 2010, and Lucy, a young woman said to have been a squatter who died from hypothermia somewhere around the Stanley.

While there's no evidence to corroborate the existence of Lucy, Estep believes he has encountered Paul. "During one tour in the Concert Hall, I heard the sound of heavy footsteps stomping across the wooden floorboards below me," Estep said, adding that he was up in the balcony at the time. "All twenty people on my tour heard the footsteps, too. Thinking that I may have been punked, I took two visitors down to the basement with me, in case somebody was banging on the ceiling above. The basement was deserted."

During the ghost tour, a woman from the Midwest said she saw a shadow figure dart behind me in the basement around the time I heard the female spirit say "open." According to Olivia, the room is often frequented by the mysterious stowaway spirit. When I walked into Lucy's hangout, a closet door slowly creaked opened.

Yes, I was legitimately creeped out by the cellar dweller. However, that brief moment was probably the most spine-tingling paranormal activity that I experienced during the entire investigation. I'm still not sure if it was Paul or Lucy that I was communicating with in the Concert Hall's basement. In hindsight, it could have been F.O. Stanley himself or his wife, Flora.

The ghostly husband-and-wife duo have been spotted roaming the halls and the lobby of the hotel, "making sure that everything is running properly," reported *Where The Ghosts Live* blog. "One year prior to F.O.'s death, his wife, Flora had a stroke in the lobby of the hotel. Having been a very accomplished piano player, it is said

The Stanley Hotel was built by Freelan Oscar Stanley and opened on July 4, 1909. PHOTO COURTESY DEPOSIT PHOTOS.

that she will still have a seat and plays a piece on the piano for her guests."

As our tour was coming to an end, I was waiting for the ghost of Flora to manifest as our group investigated the MacGregor Ballroom. Did I hear any phantom piano music? Nope. However, I did have an uneasy feeling as I walked up the stairs and came face-to-face with the painting of the hotel's matriarch leering at me as I quietly retired to my room. But that was it.

While I would say, without hesitation, that the Stanley lives up to its haunted reputation, I had to rethink my irrational fears of an ax-wielding Jack Torrance barging into my bathroom or a late-night visitation by those gruesome Grady girls.

I didn't have a "redrum" moment.

"Contrary to the contents of King's excellent novel, the Stanley has no dark or violent history," Estep told me. "It has more than one hundred years of happiness and joy, for the most part, and I believe that some of that positive emotion has remained behind after all these years and is behind many of the paranormal phenomena that visitors report."

I ended up having a peaceful night's sleep. I especially enjoyed the little touches, like having my clothing neatly unpacked and folded when I returned to my supposedly haunted room. I even woke up tucked into my bed even though I fell asleep on top of the duvet. Elizabeth Wilson sure knows how to make guests at the Stanley feel right at home.

Next time, however, I'm going to sleep with the lights on.

STEPHEN KING

Taking the SK Tours of Maine with Stu Tinker was like riding shotgun with Stephen King himself. The former bookstore owner picked me up in his black sedan outside of Paddy Murphy's, an Irish pub on the corner of Bangor's Main Street. The historic red-brick building was obviously important to Tinker.

"Right behind me was Betts, the oldest bookstore in Bangor," he explained. "I was there for twenty years. It's actually where Steve had his first official bookstore signing for *Carrie*."

Tinker initially met King in 1974 at the event and he developed a friendship with the future master of horror. King, an English teacher and struggling author at the time, became an overnight phenomenon thanks to the success of the film directed by Brian De Palma.

Meanwhile, Tinker carved out a name for himself and eventually owned and operated Betts Bookstore. The SK Tours of Maine guide is now the go-to expert when it comes to the local author. His tour spotlights King's real-life inspiration for the fictional Derry, Maine, and gives little-known details about the horror writer's philanthropic efforts within the community.

Tinker told me that King got his start in the small town of Durham before heading to college in nearby Orono, where he met his wife Tabitha. "As he grew up, his whole world was only a bike ride around Durham," Tinker explained, adding that King's father abandoned his family when King was just two. In Durham, the author found a paperback collection of H.P. Lovecraft in the attic of his childhood home. In a 2009 interview with Barnes & Noble Studios King said, "I knew that I'd found home when I read that book." Apparently Lovecraft left an indelible impression on the up-and-coming writer.

When King moved to Bangor, Tinker said he wrote several short stories but was having a difficult time making ends meet. "He told everybody since he was twelve that he was going to be a writer, but he struggled during the early days when he was living in a trailer with Tabby," said Tinker. In fact, Tabitha fished the first few pages of *Carrie* out of the garbage and offered to help her husband understand the complexities of teen girl angst. "Tabby thought the shower scene in *Carrie* was all wrong, so she brought Steve to her former all-girls school, the John Bapst Memorial High School, so he could see for himself what it was like."

After the success of the movie version of *Carrie*, King's career flourished and he eventually moved to his bat-gated mansion on West Broadway in Bangor. Tinker, who grew up in a house abutting the Thomas Hill Standpipe, told me that King would take long walks around Bangor when he was writing the 1987 horror novel that introduced Derry's boogeyman, Pennywise the Dancing Clown. In fact, King spent hours penning the book on a bench outside of Tinker's home at the top of Thomas Hill.

"When he originally wrote *It*, the story took place in Bangor," the tour guide explained. "Steve started having some concerns about offending people because what he was writing made the town sound very evil."

Tinker said King was inspired by real-life locations and actual historic events from Bangor's storied past. "We had a kid get thrown in the stream down here because he was gay," he explained. "It was the first hate crime ever in Bangor and possibly in the entire state. It was such a shock to everybody and it made Steve change the story from Bangor to this fictitious town of Derry."

Charlie Howard, a twenty-three-year-old gay man, was thrown over the State Street Bridge by three teenagers on July 7, 1984, and he drowned in the Kenduskeag Stream. The murder inspired King to write a similar scene in the beginning of *It*, where three homophobic teenagers throw an openly gay man, Adrian Mellon, over a bridge and into the Kenduskeag. In the book, Mellon was then devoured by Pennywise.

Tinker said the murder of gangster Al Brady was based on a real gun battle that happened in downtown Bangor on October 12, 1937, in the middle of Central Street, another scar from the city's dark past. The FBI fatally shot Brady and his accomplice in a blaze of gunfire. The bank robber's death ultimately led to the demise of The Brady Gang.

The Thomas Hill Standpipe, which regulates Bangor's water supply and is literally next to Tinker's home, was also woven into *It* when King alluded to the true story of a local boy who climbed into the tower and drowned. "He was sliding down the banister and he fell between the stairway and the tank," Tinker recalled. "By the time they got him out, he died."

When Tinker drove me to the infamous sewer grate on the corner of Union and Jackson Streets, he said that King was taking his usual morning walk when he noticed water draining into the sewer. Somehow the grate inspired the terrifying opening sequence of *It*.

The tour guide isn't sure how the drain became the home of the shape-shifting Pennywise who dismembered the young Georgie as he tried to retrieve the paper boat made by his big brother, Bill. However, Tinker believes that King, much like the "Losers' Club" in the book, confronts his darkest fears when he hashes out his characters.

"He always said that he writes his nightmares," Tinker said at the end of the tour. "And somehow everything he sees along the way becomes part of that nightmare."

KING'S HAUNT: CHARLES INN

BANGOR, ME—Yes, you'll float, too. Allan and Leeann Hewey, the owners of the historic Charles Inn located in the Phenix Block of downtown Bangor, wanted to honor the city's larger-than-life hero, Stephen King.

When they planned the hotel's themed rooms during renovations, the couple created two King-inspired suites based on the author's books. For example, the Derry, Maine room features movie posters from *Pet Sematary*, red balloons painted on the walls, and insider tidbits about the fictional town featured in several of the horror writer's books, including *It* and *Bag of Bones*. The inn's King's Room suite boasts items donated by the master of horror, including books from his personal library and a creepy dress form.

According to Tinker, the former owner and operator of the now closed Betts Bookstore, which was across the street from the hotel, King would send out-of-town visitors to the overnight haunt when it was called the Phenix Inn. "I would see him there often when he had celebrity guests in town like J.K. Rowling, Meg Ryan, and John Mellencamp," Tinker told me.

The basement of the Charles Inn served as a speakeasy during the Prohibition Era and was on the outskirts of Bangor's red-light district. Built in 1873, the building likely had a past life as a bordello before being turned into a hotel in 1980.

Based on the building's storied history, it should come as no surprise that it is one of the city's most haunted. "Some of the spooks include a Union soldier who was trying to help during the Civil War but paid the ultimate price," reported Amanda McDonald from Q1065-FM's blog highlighting Bangor's most paranormally active places. "Another frequent occurrence is that of a woman in white. She may be the one responsible for keeping a few of the rooms quite chilly."

Thanks to a much-need renovation from the Travel Channel television show *Hotel Impossible*, the updated rooms include memorabilia from Bangor's history, so a few of the items brought in could very well be the source of the paranormal activity. The haunted Room 305, nicknamed the "Mostly Ghostly," boasts a collection of eerie toys, and at least one of the hotel's lingering spirits, a little girl named Elizabeth, is believed to be attached to a handmade cloth doll reproduced from the Civil War era.

The haunted object was taken from nearby Fort Knox and was used to lure a four-year-old girl ghost. Jame Dube, founder of the East Coast Ghost Trackers, recently donated the trigger object to the hotel. The doll was used during his group's investigations at the fortification, which was built between 1844 and 1869.

Based on Dube's account, the child spirit was extremely interactive at Fort Knox. In fact, Elizabeth regularly moved marbles and frequently made herself known during paranormal investigations. "She likes to do that and it's very freaky for the people who are actually sitting in the chair getting touched," Dube told Shonna Narine from Bangor's WFVX in October 2017. "There are certain spots of the fort that are kind of hot spots where we know what the entities are and where we can have interaction with them."

Dube said that several psychics told him that Elizabeth is looking for her mother and doesn't know that she's dead. "She loves to interact with her dolls," Dube explained. "We've heard her voice before and it's definitely Elizabeth."

When East Coast Ghost Trackers moved the haunted item to the Charles Inn, the four-year-old ghost apparently followed it.

The Charles Inn's co-owner Leeann Hewey told Maine's NBC affiliate, WCSH-TV, that she has seen wine glasses fly across the room and has picked up a disembodied voice. "I heard this little tiny voice go 'nee nee nee nee nee,' and I looked at my husband," she explained. "I said, 'Oh, the grandkids are out in the hall.' And he goes, 'No, they're not here.' And I said, 'Do you hear that?' And he turned down the TV and I heard the same thing again, this little voice next to me, then I got completely cold."

Hewey's husband Allan claimed that several of the hotel's guests have reported phantom footsteps walking up the stairs and other mysterious things that go bump in the night. "Guests would say that somebody was knocking on the door, and they'd open the door and nobody would be there," he said.

Leann insists that her hotel is paranormally active. "Something's going on, and how do we find out what it is and get control of it so number one, it doesn't hurt our business, and number two, we don't have people thinking we're crazy, because we're not crazy," she said. "For us, it's fun. It's adventurous. It just kind of helps us to know that we're not alone."

During a recent investigation at the Charles Inn, I encountered at least two child spirits at the hotel. One was a mischievous boy ghost who moves items in the coffee shop and lobby area downstairs. In the "Most Ghostly" room, I interacted with a little girl ghost with braids. She was tugging on my shirt saying, "Mister, mister." Based on the input that I received from a group of empaths watching my online video, the girl wanted to play with one of the dolls encased in glass. Yes, she was eyeing the doll clearly marked "Property of Fort Knox."

Was the young ghost from the fort trying to get my attention? Yes, I strongly believe it was Elizabeth giggling in the shadows of Bangor's Charles Inn.

GHOST Q&A: CAROLINE BICKS

"He understood the dramatic power of ghosts and the visceral terror they could evoke."

—Caroline Bicks, Stephen E. King Chair

How often do you get the chance to compare and contrast Maine's Master of Horror with the Bard of Avon? Caroline Bicks, a Shakespeare scholar and the Stephen E. King Chair in Literature at UMaine, said King's books like *The Shining* and *Pet Semetary* do have a few things in common with the universal themes explored in *Hamlet* and *MacBeth*.

Like Shakespeare, King's books boast tragic characters, the paternal struggle between fathers and sons, and, of course, ghosts. Yes, the supernatural themes found in books like *Doctor Sleep* and *The Stand* were also explored by the Bard.

Bicks, who specializes in Shakespeare's lingering influence on popular culture, told me that it was actually King's archetypal characters that haunted her imagination when she was younger. "I grew up spending my summers in Maine with no TV and a great local library," she said. "I remember picking up *Night Shift*—I was probably eight or nine years old— and getting increasingly creeped out as I read through each story. I'm still traumatized by 'The Boogeyman' and have to keep the closet closed when I sleep."

Caroline Bicks

PHOTO COURTESY CAROLINE BICKS.

71

The *Shakespeare, Not Stirred* author also draws a parallel between the "mental puberty" that the character Carrie experiences in King's novel of the same name, and that which Juliet goes through when she nears "the change of fourteen years" at the start of *Romeo and Juliet.* After this awakening, both characters go on to "act out scenes that range from the romantic to the gruesome," she said.

In the interview, Bicks revisited the chilling ghosts from her childhood haunting the jagged Maine coastline, her take on Shakespeare's specters, and the primordial fear of the shadows lurking in our collective closet.

Q: How did the ghost lore from your summers in Castine, Maine, shape your childhood?
A: Castine is a town steeped in ghost stories—in the town cemetery, and the forts, and the old houses. And so many of my childhood memories are connected to watching and listening for them.

There's the story of the Little Drummer Boy, an American boy left behind in a dungeon of Fort George when the British abandoned it after the war of 1812. He drummed himself to death, they say. At the last full moon in August, you supposedly can hear him drumming. I never did, but we used to set up camp listening for him.

My favorite story of the supernatural is the legend of Buck's Grave in the nearby town of Bucksport. My memory is that he was the governor of the town at the height of the witch craze. He had just sentenced a woman to burn at the stake, and she cursed him while she was burning up: "I will follow you to your grave!" Her leg rolled out of the fire. And over the years, the shape of a woman's leg has been emerging and getting darker on his gravestone. We'd drive past it at the start and end of every summer, and each year the outline of the leg would get clearer. A heart lying on its side has also started to show up above the leg. That one I can testify to.

Those ghosts, and all of the history and gripping stories they carry with them, are the reason I got so interested in learning about older time periods and doing what I do today as a Shakespeare scholar.

Q: As an adult and academic, are you a believer in ghosts?
A: I am. I wasn't raised with a particular religion, so my belief in ghosts isn't connected to any institutional belief system. I believe

in a spirit world, and actually had a regular encounter with some kind of spectral presence when I was very young. It would always appear to me just as I was going to sleep. Not unlike how many of Shakespeare's ghosts appear in his plays—in that borderland between sleep and waking.

Q: What role do ghosts play in the Bard's earlier works, and did it change throughout his career?
A: When ghosts appear in the history plays, like *Richard III* or *Julius Caesar*, Shakespeare usually has morphed them into ghosts from stories that appeared in his historical sources. In *Richard III*, for instance, Richard sees the ghosts of his murder victims on the eve of the Battle of Bosworth, which is where the future King Henry VII will defeat him. They each curse him and tell him to "despair and die!" He's asleep when he sees them, but the audience sees them as well, so they occupy that ghost/dream middle-ground that Shakespeare often stages.

In the sources Shakespeare was working with, though, Richard dreams about generic devils. So in those early history plays, I think he's using ghosts to represent the process by which history gets made and authorized. Of course, Richard will be righteously murdered by the man who will found the glorious Tudor line—the ghosts have predicted it.

Q: What is your take on the Shakespearean specter in plays like *Hamlet*, *Julius Caesar*, and *MacBeth*?
A: In *Macbeth*, the ghost of Banquo does some of the same work that the ghosts in the history plays are doing. The ghost authorizes the history of the current English monarch—in this case James I, the king of Scotland who took over the throne of England when Elizabeth died. Banquo was the legendary ancestor of James, so you can see that Shakespeare is using him, like how he used the ghosts in *Richard III*, to say: "You have messed with the wrong royal line. You are going down."

Q: King was inspired to write *The Shining* after having a profound dream at the Stanley Hotel in Estes Park, Colorado. What role do dreams play in Shakespeare's plays?
A: My favorite ghost in Shakespeare is one that we don't see, but that Antigonus from *The Winter's Tale* talks about as a vision that

he saw of Hermione, the wife of the King who accused her of adultery and put her on trial.

She dies of grief, or so we are led to believe, and Antigonus is sent to take her newborn baby and leave it to die in the wilderness. He tells the audience that Hermione's spirit came to him, but he isn't sure if it was a dream or a real ghost. She tells him where to leave the baby and what to name her, and that Antigonus will never see his wife again. So, sure enough, he gets ripped apart by a bear right after leaving the baby on the shores of Bohemia. The thing is, though, Hermione isn't dead. She's been pretending to be dead.

So, what did he see? If it was just a dream, and not her actual ghost, then how did she know he was going to die? If it was a ghost, then was Shakespeare playing with time and space by having her dead and alive in parallel universes? *The Winter's Tale* was one of his last plays, and he was getting increasingly experimental with form. So I wouldn't be surprised if he was using ghosts to help him play with these out-of-the-box ideas.

Q: Are Shakespeare's specters a reflection of his time or is it something more profound?
A: What's interesting about Shakespeare's ghosts is that the characters who see them often experience them as dreams. Or they aren't sure if they're dreaming or awake. This reflects, in part, the increasing skepticism about ghosts initiated by the Protestant Reformation. Catholics believed that when you saw a ghost, it was the spirit of someone—typically a family member—who was in Purgatory for their sins, and they were coming to you begging for prayers to help get them out of there and on to Heaven. The other option was that it was a demon trying to trick you by posing as a loved one. But for many Protestants, Purgatory was considered a bunch of Popish hocus pocus, and so was the idea of a loved one's spirit coming back. That isn't to say that people didn't believe in ghosts at all. There was plenty of folklore about ghosts. They just weren't attached to the same religious apparatus.

Q: King notoriously doesn't believe in ghosts. Do you think Shakespeare was a believer? If so, why or why not?
A: I don't know. What I do know is that he understood the dramatic power of ghosts, the visceral terror they could evoke, and the ways they force confrontations with the past and with one's own sometimes tortured relationship to it.

Q: What are your thoughts regarding the Boogeyman?
A: If I think about why the Boogeyman terrified me so much as a young girl and why I still carry traces of that fear, I'd attribute it to where he lurks. A closet is such a private and everyday space. And he's invaded it. It's like you can't hide from him. That kind of monster scares me more than the Little Drummer Boy, who doesn't live in my house.

Q: What scares you?
A: Possessed children. I'm still scarred by *The Omen* and *The Exorcist*. I was watching *The Shining* again the other night, and I could barely stand the scenes where Tony starts speaking through Danny. I know that Tony isn't a demon, and isn't even trying to hurt anyone, but there's something about children disappearing into another being that just terrifies me. I think it has something to do with seeing the disjunction between trusting innocence and some kind of horrifying knowledge.

THE FAMOUS

"An idea, like a ghost, must be spoken to a little before it will explain itself."

—CHARLES DICKENS, *THE LAMPLIGHTER*

GHOST PROFILE: SUSAN WILSON

"The legend is that it's just the ghost of Dickens, messing with us."
—Susan Wilson, Omni Parker House historian

Susan Wilson, author of *Heaven, By Hotel Standards*, said it was love at first "site" when she first visited the oldest continuously operating hotel in the country, the Omni Parker House, more than twenty-five years ago.

"I was a frequent contributor for the *Boston Globe*. I had a column called 'Sites & Insights' and I would write about some location in Boston, like Fenway Park or the Boston Common," Wilson told me. "One of the featured sites was the Parker House. Every time I would do one of those *Globe* columns, I ended up knowing more about the sites than the people who actually worked there. The Parker House was so happy with what I put together. Actually, that article still hangs on the wall in the general manager's office."

Fast forward to 2012 when the hotel's staff approached the historian to help write a book on the Omni Parker House. Wilson agreed, but she had one condition. The columnist-turned-author had been helping out the hotel with research for years, but longed for an official title. She wanted to be the house historian.

"Channeling Beyoncé, I said, 'Put a ring on it' and I became the official house historian in 2012," she said with a laugh. "It's

PHOTO COURTESY SUSAN WILSON.

actually a real job. I'm only part-time because I do all sorts of things, but I work at the hotel at least one day a week."

As a self-professed history addict, she was living the dream because "the Parker House is at the epicenter of Boston history," she explained. "Being born in 1855, the hotel intersects with so many aspects of the city's past."

When asked if being the Omni Parker House's official historian was the coolest job ever, she said "yes" without hesitation. "Some say the Parker House and I were lucky to find each other because we are a really good fit."

One of the mysteries Wilson untangled regarding the hotel's past involved a celebrity French chef named Sanzian. "If he was so famous, why couldn't anybody find anything on him?" Wilson asked. Digging for information, she searched the archives at the *Globe*. Wilson was shocked to discover that the hotel was spelling the former chef's name incorrectly. "For seventy-five years, they've been writing about Sanzian, but he never existed," she recalled. "It was Anezin, not Sanzian."

Another bit of misinformation was the year the Parker House officially opened. "The plaque outside said it opened in 1856. It didn't," she said. "It took me less than a day of research to find out that it was 1855."

There's one historical gem that Wilson uncovered that may or may not be true. "When I was doing research on Harvey Parker, one article that I found said that he worked for Dr. George Parkman," she said. "When he worked in Boston, he did all sorts of odd jobs, so it's possible."

However, the official house historian told me that she couldn't corroborate the story. "I could only find a brief mention in one article," she said. "It's just too delicious of a story to dismiss, but I can't prove it."

For the record, one of the most heinous crimes from Boston's past centers on Dr. George Parkman, who was beaten and dismembered in a Harvard Medical College laboratory in 1849.

Hailing from one of the most prominent families in Boston, Parkman was a retired doctor who became a landlord and money lender in the early 1800s. Nicknamed "Old Chin," Parkman befriended one of his clients, John White Webster, who was a professor of chemistry and geology at Harvard Medical College. Incidentally, the Parkman family donated a large sum of money to fund Harvard's medical school, which was formerly located near the Mass General Hospital.

Webster borrowed $400 from Parkman, who was reported missing days following an attempt to collect his money. Bostonians were on the hunt for the missing landlord, and police printed 28,000 missing-person fliers. After a sensational trial and Webster's eventual confession, the press had a field day spitting out "Harvard Professor and Murder" headlines guaranteed to captivate the city.

On August 30, 1850, the professor was hanged at the gallows in the Boston Common.

How did Webster murder Parkman? After an unexpected collections call at Webster's laboratory, the professor took his walking stick and clubbed Parkman in the head in a fit of rage. Panicked, Webster reportedly chopped the body into pieces and threw the remains into the toilet.

In his confession, Webster claimed that it was an act of self-defense. He said that Parkman "was speaking and gesticulating in the most violent and menacing manner" about the loan. In response, Webster "seized whatever thing was handiest—it was a stick of wood—and dealt him an instantaneous blow with all the force that passion could give it. It was on the side of his head, and there was nothing to break the force of the blow. He fell instantly upon the pavement. There was no second blow. He did not move."

During the trial, a police officer testified that Parkman's torso was found in a bloodstained tea chest, which was displayed to the court. Webster also allegedly burned Parkman's bones, including his jawbone complete with false teeth, in the furnace. The officer also said that it was possible to fit the victim's remaining body parts in the toilet, but the torso wouldn't fit.

Charles Dickens, who was intrigued by the infamous murder, paid a visit to Webster's laboratory eighteen years after the trial. His response to the murder scene? The *Great Expectations* author said "the room smelled as if the body was there."

Speaking of Dickens, Wilson said the lauded British author left an indelible imprint on the Omni Parker House during his five-month stay in 1867. "Dickens had already come to the United States two times at this point. He didn't stay at the Parker House the first time because it didn't exist," she said, adding that he stayed at the Tremont Hotel in 1842. "He didn't come back for years because there was a backlash against him after wrote *American Notes,* which was somewhat critical of the states."

By 1867 Dickens was making a comeback thanks, in part, to the popularity of *A Christmas Carol*. "He was comparable to a rock star today," Wilson said. "Christmas had been banned in Boston and there was a renewed interest in the holiday. People really wanted to see him and he sold out of venues with more than 2,000 seats."

He was so popular, Wilson said, the hotel had to place armed guards outside to keep fans away while Dickens was staying there.

Wilson said the famed author of *A Tale of Two Cities* stayed at the hotel because of its status as the designated meeting place for the Saturday Club, a social and literary group started by Ralph Waldo Emerson in 1855, whose members included Henry Wadsworth Longfellow and James Russell Lowell. Its reputation as a hangout for Boston's Brahmin writers made it a natural choice for Dickens.

"It kind of brought full circle the greatest English-speaking literary person in the world and the first great American authors," she said.

Wilson said the Parker House had become the hub of Boston's literary elite because it was close to the Old Corner Bookstore and the Boston Athenaeum. "I can't emphasize location enough," she continued. "All of these amazing authors were walking up and down the street and the Parker House was at the center of it all."

When Dickens stayed at the Parker House, he practiced in front of a mirror using exaggerated voices and facial expressions giving life to the many characters featured in his stories. "Dickens was quite a theatrical character," Wilson said. "He would recite *A Christmas Carol* wearing capes and cravats. He had studied acting so he was actually a trained actor."

Wilson said the mirror that Dickens practiced in front of is now hanging in the Omni Parker House's mezzanine level. "In addition to the mirror, we have the mantle from the fireplace that was in his suite, which is now in a private conference room. Three years ago we acquired the actual door to his suite," she said, adding that the door is now in the lower level of the hotel next to the executive offices.

When I asked Wilson about the alleged hauntings associated with Dickens at the Omni Parker House, she told me that the hotel's elevator mysteriously gets called to the third floor. When the doors open, no one is there. "The legend is that it's just the ghost of Dickens, messing with us," she said.

There's also a creepy story associated with the door from Dickens's suite that's on display in the basement. "One of the staff members was standing in front of the Dickens door and said that she felt a presence behind her," Wilson told me. "It was almost like a wind or a breeze and the employee turned around and there was no one there. It happened multiple times. She thought that maybe Dickens was trying to get into his door."

Wilson said that she has never had a face-to-face encounter with the historic hotel's ghosts. "I'm just the house historian," she said. "I've personally never had a paranormal experience. I just collect the stories from others who have."

There's one story involving the hotel's namesake and founder, Harvey Parker, that has been retold to her often. "There have been claims that on the tenth-floor annex people have seen a figure hovering—with facial hair and seems to be from another era. Should

Originally built in October 1855, the Parker House boasts a slew of ghostly reports ranging from Harvey Parker himself—who passed away on May 31, 1884, at the age of seventy-nine and apparently continues to roam the halls of the hotel he built—to mysterious orbs floating down the tenth-floor corridor. PHOTO COURTESY DEPOSIT PHOTOS.

that be true, it might very well be Harvey Parker just looking over the place making sure that the guests are happy and everything is working correctly," Wilson said.

The Omni Parker House's historian said the spirit of Harvey Parker is still very much alive because of the hotel's welcoming vibe. "The thing that makes it different than the other hotels in town is the history and the ambience. It has an aura of friendliness that Parker was known for, and it still has that old-fashioned, friendly charm," she said. "If Harvey Parker's ghost isn't there, his spirit definitely is."

CHARLES DICKENS

In 1842 the Old South Meeting House made a huge impression on the internationally famous author Charles Dickens. On his first night after landing in Boston during his United States premiere, the author eagerly explored the streets of Boston with his publisher James T. Fields. Rounding the corner of School Street and heading to Washington, Dickens let out a "scream" of delight when he encountered the Old South Meeting House. Remembering the incident years later, Fields said, "To this day I cannot tell why. Was it because of its fancied resemblance to St. Paul's or the Abbey? I declare firmly, the mystery of that shout is still a mystery to me."

Inside Boston's Old South Meeting House visitors can see where Ben Franklin was baptized and, more importantly, where Samuel Adams fueled the whole "no taxation without representation" Patriot war cry against British rule.

The Boston Tea Party rally was originally slated for Faneuil Hall, but it was moved to the Old South Meeting House because that building was large enough to handle the spill-over masses. At the time, it was the largest building in colonial Boston. Old South was also where thousands of outraged Bostonians gathered to protest the Boston Massacre in March 1770, in which five colonists were killed by British soldiers.

Built in 1729 by a Puritan congregation who probably had no idea that this Freedom Trail favorite would play such an important role in American history. It was the go-to gathering place of record for more than three centuries; the Old South Meeting House is also reportedly haunted.

Michael Baker, investigator with Para-Boston, organized a paranormal investigation at the historic building. Their findings? The paranormal investigation team did record an EVP (electromagnetic voice phenomenon) of a male voice saying, "Who's there?" There were also first-hand accounts of chains rattling in the lower area of the Old South Meeting House and a bizarre recording anomaly coming from the building's steeple.

Was any evidence discovered of a Revolutionary War–era horse spirit lingering in the building, as some have suggested? Nay . . . or should that be "neigghhhh." Unless the EVP was of a dead Mr. Ed. However, several visitors to the building have reported smelling hay, and one woman who recently tied the knot in the Old South Meeting House said she had a close encounter with the horse spirit.

For the record, the Redcoats ransacked the building during the Revolutionary War and used it as a horse stable and riding school for British soldiers. George Washington walked by the building during the late 1700s and was extremely unhappy with how the Brits had desecrated this important landmark.

During his second visit to Boston, Dickens stayed in what is now the oldest continuously operating hotel in the country, the Omni Parker House. Besides being one of the more breathtakingly ornate structures in Boston, Dickens's old haunt is also allegedly one of its most haunted. Originally built in October 1855, the Parker House boasts a slew of ghostly reports ranging from a sighting of the spirit of Harvey Parker himself—who passed away on May 31, 1884, at the age of seventy-nine and apparently continues to roam the halls of the hotel he built—to mysterious orbs floating down the tenth-floor corridor and a malevolent male spirit with a disturbing laugh who reportedly lingers in room 303.

Parker's rags-to-riches story started in 1826, when he moved to Boston with nothing but a pocket full of change. He saved his nickels and dimes while working as a coachman for a Brahmin socialite and built a restaurant that later became his namesake hotel. Torn down, except for one wing, and rebuilt in its present gilded glory in the late 1920s, the hotel was called the Parker House until the 1990s, when the Omni hotel chain purchased the Victorian structure.

The hotel has several claims to fame, including being the birthplace of the Boston cream pie. It's also had a few famous employees, including Ho Chi Minh, who was a busboy; and Malcolm X, who worked as a waiter. John Wilkes Booth stayed at the Parker House eight days before assassinating President Lincoln on April 14, 1865. In fact, he used a shooting gallery not far from the hotel to practice his aim before heading to Ford's Theatre in Washington, D.C.

Other haunted happenings have involved elevators mysteriously being called to the third floor—once frequented by both Dickens and Henry Wadsworth Longfellow. The hotel's ornate lifts are known to mysteriously stop on the floor without anyone pushing a button.

On the mezzanine level of the hotel, next to the pressroom where John F. Kennedy announced his candidacy for president, is the so-called "enchanted mirror," which was taken from *A Christmas Carol* author's room and is known to do odd things when guests say "Charles Dickens" three times. "This mirror is the one that Charles Dickens used to practice his orations in front of," said Jeffrey Doucette, a former ghost tour guide. "Not long ago, a worker began to clean the mirror, and he kept seeing condensation appear on the glass right next to him, as if someone was breathing on it. He hasn't cleaned the glass since."

Compared to his first visit to Boston in the 1840s, Dickens's 1867 visit was a less public affair. Fans once again thronged the docks—this time in East Boston—waiting for his ship, but Dickens's English manager, George Dolby, had a Custom House tugboat fetch the author and take him undetected to Long Wharf. The Parker House hotel arranged for Dickens to use a back staircase during his stay, and while the author happily reconnected with old friends, he declined many other social invitations.

His performances, however, were inarguably a triumph, with his December 24, 1867, reading of *A Christmas Carol* at the Tremont Temple being a highlight. "I never saw anything like them on Christmas Eve," Dickens wrote home about the Boston crowd. He earned $25,000, an astounding sum at the time, from the sold-out tour, which encompassed eighteen American cities, but the experience left him physically depleted.

Two years after returning home, while working on the *Mystery of Edwin Drood*, he died of a stroke on June 9, 1870. In Boston, those present for his reading in the Tremont Theatre had heard his final goodbye to a city that had become a "memorable and beloved spot" for him. "Ladies and Gentlemen—I beg most earnestly, most gratefully, and most affectionately to bid you each and all farewell."

DICKENS'S HAUNT: BOSTON COMMON

BOSTON, MA—"There are bodies everywhere," I said during a recording of the Biography Channel show *Haunted Encounters: Face To Face* in 2012. "The spot where he had the initial encounter was a mass gravesite."

I was standing in front of Boylston and Tremont, an area I've identified as Boston's haunted corridor thanks to an aura of disaster imprinted by the gas line explosion of 1897.

Beginning as a sheep and cow pasture, the forty-eight-acre Boston Common was originally purchased from Boston's first settler, William Blackstone, in 1634. Now touted as the oldest city park in the United States, it's also home to some of the darker chapters from Boston's not-so-Puritanical past.

The Boston Common is chock-full of ghosts, graves, and gallows. It is, in essence, "one big anonymous burying ground," wrote Holly Nadler, author of *Ghosts of Boston Town*. "Under the Puritan regime, untold numbers of miscreants—murderers, thieves, pirates, Indians, deserters, Quakers, and putative witches—were executed in the Common" at the so-called Great Elm, which was also nicknamed the hanging tree or gallows tree by locals. "At risk to their own lives, friends and family might sneak in under the cover of darkness, cut down the cadaver and bury it somewhere in the park," continued Nadler. "If no one came forward to deal with the disastrous remains, town officials disposed of them in the river, where bloated bodies frequently washed in and out with the tides."

There was also a mass grave site near the southern corner of the Common, yards away from the designated Central Burying Ground. In early 1895, the human remains of one hundred dead bodies were uncovered during the excavation of the nation's first underground trolley station, now the Boylston Green Line stop. A mob scene of "curiosity seekers" lined up along the Boylston Street corner of the Common "looking at the upturning of the soil," according to the April 18, 1895, edition of the *Boston Daily Globe*. The report continued, saying that "a large number of human bones and skulls are being unearthed as the digging on the Boylston Street mall" progressed. Thrill-seeking spectators were horrified by the sights and smells emanating from the site and were forced to move by early May.

And that was just the first round of skeletons in the Common's collective closet. As the excavation continued, officials uncovered the remains of hundreds—some historians estimated between 900 and 1,100 bodies—buried in shallow graves beneath the Boylston mall.

While the nearby Granary Burial Ground earns top billing thanks to its Freedom Trail–friendly names, including Paul Revere, Samuel Adams, John Hancock, and even Mother Goose, the Boston Common's lesser-known Central Burying Ground has something that the other graveyards don't: ghosts. After Boston's Puritan leaders purchased the plot in 1756, the cemetery was used as a final resting spot for foreigners and other paupers who couldn't cough up enough shillings for a proper burial. The graveyard is the resting spot for composer William Billings, and artist Gilbert Stuart, who was responsible for painting George Washington's mug on the dollar bill. It is also reportedly the place where the see-through denizens from the Common's spirit realm prefer to hang out.

"Visitors to the graveyard have reported seeing shadowy figures appear nearby, often near trees," wrote Christopher Forest in *Boston's Haunted History*. "The figures disappear or dissolve when people look right at them. Some people have associated the figures with the former hanging victims who met their end on the Boston Common gallows."

Apparently the cemetery's spirits like to have fun with tourists. "They have been accused of poking people in the back, rattling keys and even brushing up against shoulders. Some people roaming the graveyard have reported being grabbed from behind by an unseen force," Forest wrote.

Jeffrey Doucette, a veteran tour guide, said he was a skeptic until he witnessed a woman have a close encounter with a paranormal force outside the cemetery's gates in 2011. "She felt someone or something tap her on the shoulder," he said. "She looked annoyed, and I had to assure her that no one was there."

The more notorious haunting at the Central Burying Ground centers on a young female spirit who was described by the late ghost expert Jim

McCabe as a teen girl "with long red hair, sunken cheekbones and a mud-splattered gray dress on." On a rainy afternoon in the 1970s, she paid a visit to a dentist named Dr. Matt Rutger, who reportedly experienced "a total deviation from reality as most of us know it." According to Nadler's *Ghosts of Boston Town*, Rutger was checking out the gravestone carvings. He felt a tap on his shoulder and then a violent yank on his collar. No one was there.

As Rutger was bolting from the cemetery, he noticed something out of the corner of his eye. "I saw a young girl standing motionless in the rear corner of the cemetery, staring at me intently," he said. The mischievous spirit then reappeared near the graveyard's gate, almost fifty yards from the initial encounter. Then the unthinkable happened. "He somehow made it by her to Boylston Street, and even though he couldn't see her, he felt her hand slip inside his coat pocket, take out his keys and dangle them in midair before dropping them," McCabe recounted.

Rutger, in an interview with Nadler, said the 1970s-era paranormal encounter had left an indelible mark on his psyche. "One thing is certain, the encounter affected me in very profound ways," he reflected. "As a trained medical professional, I have always seen the world in fairly empirical terms. There's no way something like that cannot completely change how you think about the world."

One Sunday evening, I scheduled an interview with ghost tour guide Jeffrey Doucette. I was waiting for him at Parker's Bar at the Omni Parker House when, after giving a ghost tour to a group of high school students from Vermont, he rushed in.

"You're not going to believe what just happened," he said. "As I was telling a story at the site of the hanging elm, I could tell something was up." Packing up his lantern and sitting down at a cozy table near the bar's fireplace, he continued, "The chaperone is waving at me as if 'Jeff, you need to look at this,' and she shows me her camera. I literally couldn't believe what I was seeing. In the photo, it looks like seven nooses hanging from the trees in the area near what was the hanging tree."

Doucette, a popular tour guide among out-of-town visitors thanks to his distinct Boston accent, said he was a skeptic for years. Then he had a few close encounters of the paranormal kind while trudging through haunted sites throughout the Boston Common and Beacon Hill. Now, he's a full-fledged believer. "I was like, 'What the...? Let's get out of here,'" he said, referring to the noose photo taken earlier in the evening and to creepy pictures of demonic, red-colored orbs shot in the Central Burying Ground. "It literally freaked me out. This year, I've seen a lot of orbs, but nothing like what I just saw. I'm not sure if [the spirits] heard me talking about the interview I'm having with you, but they really showed their colors tonight. The ghosts in the Boston Common were out in full force, and they were screaming."

Doucette was an amused skeptic until he gave his first Boston Common tour in 2009. "A kid on the tour shot a photo of me, and there were all of these white orbs near the Great Elm site," he explained. "The last photo really threw me for a loop. It was of me with a green light coming out of my belly, and I was freaked out. Since then, we've had a few orbs here and there, but this year has been out of control. Tonight, I really don't know what happened. Will I sleep? I don't know. But it was something that I've never experienced before."

The tour guide said he reached out to a psychic who told him that the green light emanating from his torso was an indication that the spirits in the Boston Common liked the way he told their stories. "At the hanging elm, many of the people who were hanged there were done so unjustifiably by the Puritans for crimes they didn't commit. If anyone disagreed with the status quo at that time, they were executed. Boston was founded by Puritans, and it was either their way or the highway ... or the hangman's noose. Even in the modern age, if you disagree with authority, there's the chance that you can be shamed. In my opinion, many of those hanged in the Boston Common were victims of [the denial of] freedom of speech and died at the hands of oppressive authority figures. So when I say on the tour that many of the people hanged at the Great Elm site died innocently, I feel like I'm giving them a voice."

Doucette continued, "I've always been respectful of the spirits in the Boston Common. They've never bothered me at home, and I never had an issue with a haunting. But j98when I do the tours, they do come out. I've been a strong advocate for those who were disenfranchised and oppressed, especially women, and they always respond to the stories that I tell on the tour."

As far as historical figures are concerned, Doucette said he's drawn to people like Ann "Goody" Glover, who was hanged on November 16, 1688 for allegedly practicing witchcraft. Glover, a self-sufficient, strong-willed Irish woman who spoke fluent Gaelic, lived in the North End, where she washed laundry for John Goodwin and his family. After a spirited spat in her native Gaelic tongue with Goodwin's thirteen-year-old daughter, Martha, Glover was accused of bewitching the four children in the household and was sent to prison for practicing the dark arts.

While Glover was exonerated of her crimes in 1988 and dubbed a "Catholic martyr" three-hundred years after her execution, Doucette said he's compelled to tell her story. However, he's not convinced that Glover's spirit is haunting the Boston Common. "People want a big name to associate with the hauntings in the Common, but I seriously don't think that's the case," he said, adding that "it makes for good storytelling."

Doucette, who ends the Haunted Boston ghost tour at the historic Omni Parker House, said he's heard many creepy tales while hanging out at Parker's Bar. "I spend a huge amount of time here," he remarked. "There was a night in October, and I came into the bar before a tour. A woman who was in her mid-fifties and working the bar asked if I gave the haunted tour and then told me the creepiest story."

According to the Parker's Bar worker, one guest checked in but had a hard time checking out. There was an early-season snowstorm, and the Parker House guest refused to pay his hotel bill. "As he was leaving and coming out of the School Street entrance, the doormat mysteriously flies up and blocks the exit as he's trying to leave," the tour guide mused. "The guy turns around and pays his bill."

Like Doucette, the man who tried to leave the Parker House without paying his bill was smacked in the face with what could have been a ghost from Boston's past. "Our history has many skeletons in its closet, and the spirits want their story to be told," he said.

HENRY DAVID THOREAU

What was going on in Henry David Thoreau's mind during his time secluded in the cabin immortalized in the book, *Walden?* The notorious bachelor decried heterosexual sex and marriage while obsessing over a crew of nude male swimmers and phallic-shaped plants surrounding his cabin in Concord, Massachusetts. In fact, Thoreau historian Jonathan Katz claims the author's "actions and words . . . indicate a specific sexual interest in members of his own sex."

The nature boy's extensive collection of classical homoerotic literature and his blatant affection for a certain Walden Pond visitor and Canadian woodchopper, Alek Therian, suggested a secret yearning to live his life authentically.

What does Thoreau's sexual orientation have to do with anything? If he was struggling with the anxiety and guilt associated with homosexual desire up until his death on May 6, 1862, then it's possible that his internal conflict would continue in the afterlife.

But if Thoreau's ghost is still sticking around, where is he? The obvious choice would be the iconic cabin in the woods. However, as *Storied Waters* author David A. Van Wie mused online in his essay, "Chasing Thoreau's Ghost," he's probably not hanging out at his former haunt.

"As much as he enjoyed living 'deliberately' in a one-room, rustic cabin, would Henry want to hole up there for the next 150 years? The cabin no longer exists, although archaeologists eventually found the footings of the chimney," Van Wie wrote. "They have a cabin replica at the Walden Pond Reservation, but I doubt very much his ghost would be there. Maybe a replica ghost?"

Van Wie's quest to find the famed transcendentalist's spirit led him to the Concord River. In his book, *A Week on the Concord and Merrimack Rivers,* Thoreau journeyed with his brother John, who died of tetanus only three years after the adventure in 1839. Thoreau wrote *A Week*, in part, as a tribute to his brother's memory.

"John's death deeply affected Henry, so the book was very important to him. He wrote the first draft of *A Week* while living at Walden Pond, and it was published five years before *Walden*," Van Wie wrote. "My guess is that if I were to encounter Henry's ghost, it would be on the Concord River, paddling with John on an eternal, joyful outing, there on the waters close to home."

While Van Wie's theory is a good one, I would suggest Concord's Colonial Inn as a possible postmortem hangout for the ghost of Thoreau. He stayed in the building when he attended Harvard from 1835 to 1837. Also, the boutique hotel was renamed the Thoreau House after Henry's aunts, the "Thoreau Girls," in the mid-1800s.

There's even a resident spirit at Concord's Colonial Inn that fits Thoreau's description. "Room 24, which is in the oldest part of the inn, is reportedly haunted," Peter Muise posted in "Concord's Haunted Inn" on his website, *New England Folklore*. A man wearing old-school clothing has been seen repeatedly in that room. "He never harms anyone or speaks, but simply walks toward the fireplace and disappears," Muise wrote.

Judith Fellenz, from Highland Falls, New York, had a similar encounter in Room 24 back in 1966. "As I opened my eyes, I saw a grayish figure at the side of my bed, to the left, about four feet away," Fellenz recalled. "It was not a distinct person, but a shadowy mass in the shape of a standing figure. It remained still for a moment, then slowly floated to the foot of the bed, in front of the fireplace. After pausing a few seconds, the apparition slowly melted away. It was a terrifying experience. I was so frightened I could not scream."

There's even a story from Thomas D'Agostino in *Haunted New England* about a group of paranormal investigators who checked out the paranormally active room in 2005. Members of the team saw a full-bodied apparition of a man wearing old-school attire. And, get this, the ghost threw a book at the investigators.

No word if the tome that inexplicably flew off the shelf was Thoreau's *Walden*.

THOREAU'S HAUNT: DOGTOWN

GLOUCESTER, MA—Henry David Thoreau toured Cape Ann with his friend John Russell during the summer of 1858. During his visit, he walked through Dogtown in Gloucester, Massachusetts, and remarked that the Babson Boulders scattered throughout the abandoned ghost town "was the most peculiar scenery of the Cape."

Author Peter Muise explores the mysteries of Cape Ann's Dogtown in *Legends and Lore of the North Shore*:

There are two words that best describe Dogtown: *magical* and *unsettling*. Officially called Dogtown Common, this remote area is located between Gloucester and Rockport on Massachusetts's Cape Ann. Miles inland from the popular beaches and bustling towns, its three-thousand acres are filled with woods, swamps, huge boulders, and a large reservoir. It's a vast expanse of rugged natural beauty.

It's also an area with a long, strange history. Dogtown's woods are filled with the ruins of long abandoned houses. Its boulders are carved with unusual mottoes. A small marker commemorates a man's unusual death. Dogtown's history is one filled with witchcraft, decay, weird occurrences, and maybe even a werewolf.

Sadly, Dogtown was also the site of a gruesome murder in the early eighties. It happened on June 24, 1984, when schoolteacher Ann Natti was brutally killed by Peter Hodgkins. Natti had left her Gloucester home that morning to meet a friend in Rockport, and decided to walk there through Dogtown. Natti was unaware that she was being watched by Hodgkins, who was part of a long-established Gloucester family but had a history of psychiatric problems.

Hodgkins silently approached Natti from behind and pushed her to the ground. He then bludgeoned her in the head with a stone and pulled off her clothes. Seeming to suddenly realize what he had done, Hodgkins fled the area in a panic, leaving Natti face-down in the mud to die from her injuries. After her body was discovered, Gloucester police quickly searched for Hodgkins, who had exposed himself to women in Dogtown in the past. Hodgkins was arrested on June 29, confessed to the crime, and was sentenced to life in prison without parole. It was a gruesome murder that shocked the Gloucester community, and colored people's perceptions of Dogtown for many years.

Hodgkins was interviewed in Elyssa East's *Dogtown: Death and Enchantment in a New England Ghost Town*. "Something calls to me," the murderer wrote in a letter to East. He said Dogtown had a significant effect on his life. "The trees are calling me near. I have to find out why. The gentle voices I hear . . . draw me to going to the woods. I would hear the elders of the trees speaking to me. I often escape there in my dreams."

Dogtown's history started optimistically in 1721, when the leaders of Gloucester opened up the interior of Cape Ann for settlement. When the Cape had been settled in the early 1600s, its center had been densely forested, but over time the trees had been cut down to make ships and buildings. This newly cleared area was dubbed the Commons Settlement.

Many new residents flocked to the Commons Settlement. The area was quite rocky and poorly suited to farming, but craftsmen established their workshops and homes there. Blacksmiths, millers, and barrel makers plied their trades while sheep and cows grazed peacefully among the area's huge boulders. The people living in the Commons were known for their hard work and industry.

That all changed during the Revolutionary War. The population dwindled when the Commons men were called away to fight, and it grew even smaller when Gloucester's church was relocated. This might seem minor to a modern reader, but churches were an important part of Colonial life. The Commons Settlement was originally established near Gloucester's church, but the city's wealthier residents arranged for the church to be relocated closer to their waterfront homes. In just a few years the Commons Settlement had changed from a thriving village to an under-populated backwater.

A few people remained in the Commons, mainly widows and other outcast women who took over its abandoned houses. Freed slaves also found refuge there. Packs of semi-feral dogs roamed through the village's streets, causing people in Gloucester to give it the derogatory nickname Dogtown. The name has stuck ever since.

Many of the Dogtown women survived by working as herbalists and fortune-tellers. For example, Rachel Rich foretold future events by looking at coffee grounds and sold a healing tonic made from foxberry leaves and spruce tops. Her daughter Becky earned her keep telling fortunes by reading tea leaves, while another woman named Daffy Archer supposedly sold medicine made from snail mucus.

Naturally, these women developed reputations as witches. It was a sinister reputation that some exploited for their own gain. Molly Jacobs worked as a fortune-teller, but also threatened to curse people who didn't give her money. Luce George did the same, but the most feared witch in Dogtown was her niece Thomazine "Tammy" Younger.

Tammy Younger lived in a dilapidated house on the main road through Dogtown. Whenever she heard travelers approaching she would stick her head out her window and curse them with her baleful gaze (and her foul language). People gave her money, food, or anything else she wanted to get her to reverse the curse.

Even after her death she filled the people of Gloucester with fear. When she died in 1821 her nephew asked cabinet-maker John Hodgkins to make her a coffin. The Hodgkins family was used to having coffins in their home, but Younger's coffin filled Mrs. Hodgkins and her children with unnatural fear. Mrs. Hodgkins felt a strange chill and thought it was caused by the woman's spirit, even though the coffin was still empty. Only when the coffin was moved into the barn did the family rest easy.

By the 1830s Dogtown was almost completely abandoned and its last resident, a freed slave named Cornelius Finson, died in February 1839. Shortly before his death Finson was found by Gloucester's sheriff in the cellar of Molly Jacobs's empty house digging in the frozen ground for buried treasure. Finson was half-starved and suffering from frostbite, so the sheriff brought him to Gloucester. He died a few days later.

Dogtown's reputation grew even more unsavory after this. Now a ghost town, its houses collapsed and its pasture became overgrown. People remembered it as a desolate village of witches, not as the hard-working Commons Settlement.

A sailor named James Merry added to the legend of Dogtown one night in 1891. He had recently traveled to Spain, and was regaling friends with tales of the bullfights he had seen. Someone mentioned a young bull they had seen in a meadow near Dogtown and dared Merry to wrestle it.

Merry was big, strong, and very drunk that night, so he agreed. The men walked to the meadow, where Merry successfully wrestled the animal to the ground.

Merry would have been remembered as just another drunk if his story ended there. But it doesn't. One year later, on the night of September 10, 1892, Merry once again walked to the pasture to wrestle the same bull. This time he went alone and the bull, now hundreds of pounds heavier, gored him. His body was found in the meadow the following day. Merry's friends put up two small markers commemorating his battles with the bull, and they remain in Dogtown to this day.

The late Robert Ellis Cahill, a former Salem sheriff and collector of strange tales, wondered if something other than a bull might have killed Merry. The man was found with his throat slashed, which seems unusual for a bull attack. The moon was full the night Merry died. Could he have been killed by a werewolf?

The question sounds ridiculous, but Cahill explained his reasoning in a small book called *New England's Things That Go Bump in the Night* (1989). According to Cahill, the Native Americans who originally lived on Cape Ann said they were descended from dog-headed men. He also claimed they believed the wolfsbane plant transformed anyone who ate it into a wolf. For the record, wolfsbane is very poisonous, so don't eat it. I haven't seen this folklore mentioned anywhere else, so I can't vouch for its authenticity.

However a large mysterious animal has been seen in Dogtown for centuries. In 1879 a man named Amos Pillsbury saw a strange creature in the woods one night. Pillsbury said "its eyes were like fire coals, and it ran past me through the bushes . . . with every hair whistling like a bell." Pillsbury's grandmother had told him stories of this monster when he was young, but he doubted her until he saw it with his own eyes. A group of men searched the woods, but the wolf-like creature was never found.

Was it the same creature that was sighted around Cape Ann in March of 1984? Some witnesses thought it might be a mountain lion, but the big cats have been extinct in Massachusetts for centuries. The creature was initially seen on a beach, but was last sighted on March 21 running down Gloucester's Raynard Street into Dogtown. It was described as a "gray monstrous dog-like animal . . . It had big teeth and was foaming at the mouth."

You can see why Dogtown has such a strange reputation, but in the 1930s the wealthy financier and Gloucester native Roger Babson tried to rehabilitate Dogtown's image. He hired unemployed masons to carve motivational slogans on its boulders. He hoped mottoes like *"Be On Time,"* *"Get a Job,"* and *"Help Mother"* would remind visitors of the hard-working people who founded the Commons Settlement. The twenty-three carved boulders still remain, hidden in the dense forest, but I think visitors will find they just add to Dogtown's uncanny atmosphere.

These Dogtown legends have a certain spooky charm, and conjure up images of Massachusetts's historic past. In contrast, Ann Natti's murder was senseless and brutal. It's hard to reconcile the magical old folklore with the harshness of modern crime, but they exist side by side in New England. Bring a friend if you decide to explore Dogtown, because it's large, isolated, and easy to get lost in. It's magical and unsettling, but sometimes there are scarier things in the woods than witches, werewolves, and ghosts.

MARK TWAIN

If there was an award for the author with the largest number of associated hauntings, it would easily go to Samuel Clemens's alter-ego, Mark Twain.

The Missouri-bred author traveled extensively on the lecture circuit, so his chances for out-of-the-ordinary experiences from the road were relatively high. When he visited the Windsor Hotel in Montréal, for example, he noticed a woman he'd met more than twenty years earlier from Carson City, Nevada. During a reception for the author in the Canadian hotel's posh drawing room, he distinctly remembered her because he got "a full front view of her face," he said in an interview with *Harper's Magazine*.

Not so odd, right? Just wait.

Later that evening, Twain lectured again and noticed his friend from Nevada. When he mentioned to the woman that he saw her earlier that day, she was astonished. "I was not at the reception," she told Twain. Apparently, the woman had just arrived in Québec about an hour before his evening event. His strange experience in Canada fascinated the *Adventures of Huckleberry Finn* author. Was it mental telegraphy? Twain called it "thought transference" and the episode at the Windsor Hotel in Montréal heightened his interest in the unexplained.

Speaking of hotels, Twain frequented Boston's Omni Parker House according to Susan Wilson, author of *Heaven, By Hotel Standards*. Believed to be one of New England's most haunted locations since opening its doors in October 1855, the oldest continuously operating hotel in the country has been home to various sightings of the apparition of the hotel's founder, Harvey Parker, who reportedly has been spotted roaming the tenth-floor annex, checking up on unsuspecting guests.

Other spooky happenings involve elevators mysteriously being called to the third floor—once frequented by both Charles Dickens and Henry Wadsworth Longfellow. That's also where the gender-bending lesbian actress, Charlotte Cushman, and an unnamed businessman died. In fact, one third-floor guestroom—the mythic room 303—was converted into a closet after unexplained reports of raucous laughter and the smell of whiskey spooked management.

Cushman, a revered Shakespearean actress who played both female and male roles, including Romeo and Cardinal Wolsey in *Henry VIII*, passed away at the hotel in 1869 after having a tumultuous relationship with sculptor Emma Stebbins.

Twain would stay at the Parker House when he lectured in the Boston area. "All kinds of impressive people came to the Saturday Club at the Parker House, including Twain," explained Wilson, adding that Twain's friend William Dean Howells, founder of *The Atlantic*, invited him to join the elite group of Brahmins. "A lot of the regulars didn't think much of Twain," Wilson told me. "I hate to say this, but they didn't have much respect for anyone outside of New England. He was a hillbilly to them."

Wilson *was* inspired by Twain, however. During one of his extended stays in Room 168 at the haunted hotel, he was interviewed by the *Boston Globe*. "Twain had his back to the reporter and was in a swivel chair with a cigar in one hand and a newspaper in another," Wilson explained. After a dramatic pause, Twain responded to the reporter. "You see for yourself that I'm pretty near heaven—not theologically, of course, but by the hotel standard," he said. Inspired by the jocular comment, Wilson named her book *Heaven, By Hotel Standards*.

There's also Twain's famous former residence in New York City. He lived in the brownstone located at 14 West Tenth Street from 1900 to 1901 and reportedly had a few inexplicable encounters during his brief-but-memorable stay there. It's been called the most haunted building in Manhattan and, based on its storied history, rightfully so. The structure near Washington Square Park is supposedly home to at least twenty-two ghosts. And if that's not enough to scare prospective tenants away, local newspapers have dubbed it "The House of Death."

There have been a series of gruesome incidents there, including a murder-suicide and tragic death of a six-year-old girl who was killed by her adopted father, Joel Steinberg, in 1987.

The full-bodied apparition of Twain himself—white suit and all—was spotted in the 1930s on the first floor near the staircase. A mother and daughter claimed they saw the ghost of the *Tom Sawyer* author and he allegedly had some unfinished business. "My name is Clemens and I have a problem here I gotta settle," the spirit supposedly told the two women. He then ascended up the stairs and disappeared.

Soon after the Twain sighting, the single-family home was converted into apartments. Actress Jan Bryant Bartell moved into one on the top floor in 1957. As soon as she walked in, Bartell felt a "monstrous moving shadow that loomed up behind her." In a memoir published years later, the woman said she felt something brush up against the back of her neck and smelled a rotting odor throughout her home. Bartell also saw a full-bodied apparition of a man in the building and he disappeared when she reached out to touch him.

Maybe Twain was making a postmortem return to NYC's murder house?

TWAIN'S HAUNT: MARK TWAIN HOUSE

HARTFORD, CT—As soon as I walked into the Mark Twain House in Hartford, Connecticut, I heard a female voice whisper "Sam," in my ear. It took me a few minutes to process that initial paranormal experience in the American High Gothic-style home.

Was the spirit reaching out to the building's former owner, Samuel Clemens?

Based on the ghostly greeting that afternoon in January 2019, my guess was that the whispering woman was referring to Twain's given first name, but I wasn't completely convinced. To be frank, it was a bit disconcerting to hear a disembodied voice call out to me. However, it's less creepy to think the ghostly inquiry was directed toward the renowned author of *The Adventures of Tom Sawyer*.

Our tour guide, Grace, told me she hadn't had a paranormal experience in the home formerly inhabited by the Clemens family from 1874 to 1891. "Many people ask if the house is haunted," Grace said when we explored the first floor of the historic property. "We do ghost tours in

October and some people believe that there are ghosts and this place is haunted," she explained.

Apparently, my question about the structure's alleged haunting made the tour guide feel uncomfortable. Grace under fire? "I've never seen a ghost here," she said with a nervous laugh. "I don't want there to be ghosts because I have to walk around the property at night. But you'll hear different things."

Some of the ghostly reports were in response to the SyFy Channel's *Ghost Hunters* investigation that premiered on December 2, 2009. The Clemens family—Twain's wife Olivia and their three children—lived in the Hartford home for seventeen years until his twenty-four-year-old daughter Susy died from meningitis in 1896. Clemens also lost his first-born child Langdon from diphtheria on June 2, 1872. Twain's only son was eighteen months when he died.

Twain and his family were heartbroken when Susy passed. They sold the Hartford estate while living in Europe and never returned to their beloved homestead. After Twain's death on April 21, 1910, the building served as a boarding school and library before becoming a museum honoring Clemens's legacy.

The house museum's staff remained relatively hush-hush about the building's hauntings until The Atlantic Paranormal Society, better known as TAPS, investigated in 2009. "There have been reports of employees and visitors seeing the apparition of a young woman in a long white dress roaming the halls and ghostly faces in the windows," reported the website *Damned Connecticut*. "Others have had their clothes tugged by unseen forces and heard the laughter of children, whispers, and other unexplained noises."

The TAPS investigation was definitely spirited. The crew heard ghostly voices and phantom footsteps. Also, an orb of light moved from the master bedroom to Susy's room. Another odd occurrence was when most of the evidence from the investigation was lost because of a computer malfunction. Luckily some of the audio was recovered, but the TAPS team had to rely on first-hand accounts from the investigators coupled with a recording of a loud thud coming from the second floor.

Once the *Ghost Hunters* episode aired on the SyFy Channel, others came out of the paranormal closet with their own personal experiences. "I went on the house tour on August 25, 2013. When we got to the top floor, in the room where he would play pool with his friends, I distinctly saw Twain, in his full regalia, standing out on the upper porch accompanied with a strong cigar smell," reported RPM on *Damned Connecticut*. "He was looking over the property with a casual and pleasant, though intense, demeanor."

One contributor, Max, claimed that he had a paranormal experience at the Mark Twain House in the 1980s. "When we came to the children's room, I said that I did not want to go in there," he remembered. "I felt something very negative that seemed to be in the two dolls placed in the chairs. We did eventually go through the room, but I practically ran through it."

According to another commenter, Barbara, the employees at the non-profit weren't allowed to discuss the hauntings. "The museum didn't want a 'haunted house' reputation," she wrote. "Many local paranormal groups have gotten contacted for years and years by visitors who have had paranormal experiences during their trip to the museum."

Ultimately, Barbara believes that Twain would have liked the television show and ghost tours. "If you know anything about Twain, you would know he absolutely loved attention whether it was good or bad," she concluded.

Is the Mark Twain House haunted? Yes. Would Twain enjoy all of the hoopla involving the ghosts haunting his former home in Hartford? Probably. As the famous author eloquently said, "You can't depend on your eyes when your imagination is out of focus."

KURT VONNEGUT

While Kurt Vonnegut didn't necessarily write about ghosts, he created a science-fiction-fueled fantasy world with paranormal-themed characters like the alien race known as the Tralfamadorians in his contemporary satire, *Slaughterhouse-Five*.

Written in a nonlinear style, his anti-war novel follows Billy Pilgrim, an unreliable narrator who believed he was held in an alien zoo and experienced time travel. On his daughter's wedding night, for example, Pilgrim was supposedly captured by an alien spaceship and taken to a planet called Tralfamadore light-years away.

He then was transported back to Earth through a time warp and ends up in 1968 New York City. Pilgrim scored a slot on a local radio show and then got kicked out because his out-of-the-world story seemed too far-fetched.

While *Slaughterhouse-Five* technically ended when the protagonist traveled back in time to WWII-era Dresden, the nonlinear storyline implies that Pilgrim dies in 1976 after giving a speech in a baseball stadium in which he foreshadows his ultimate demise. "If you think death is a terrible thing, then you have not understood a word I've said," Pilgrim announced to the crowd.

Born and raised in Indiana, Vonnegut attended Cornell University but dropped out in 1943 to join the Army. He was captured by the Germans during World War II and, when the Allied forces bombed Dresden, Vonnegut took refuge in a meat locker of the slaughterhouse where he was imprisoned.

In 1951 he quit his marketing job at General Electric in New York and moved his family to Cape Cod, Massachusetts, where he became a full-time writer. Vonnegut initially wrote articles for *Collier's* and *The Saturday Evening Post*, and opened a Saab dealership, which eventually failed.

"I believe my failure as a dealer so long ago explains what would otherwise remain a mystery: why the Swedes have never given me a Nobel Prize for literature," the author jokingly said years later.

Vonnegut emerged as a celebrated novelist and essayist in the sixties after writing the classic *Cat's Cradle* in 1963. When *Slaughterhouse-Five* was published in 1969, Vonnegut was catapulted into the spotlight and he was hailed a hero of the burgeoning anti-war movement.

While living on Scudder Lane in Cape Cod's Barnstable, Vonnegut offered advice to a crowd of students at the local high school. "He told them not to become writers because there were already too many," recalled Robin Smith Johnson in the *Cape Cod Times*. "He mentioned that F. Scott Fitzgerald was an alcoholic, Ernest Hemingway was suicidal, and Mark Twain was consumed with bitterness. He also said a writer's life was lonely, with the only person he saw everyday being his mailman."

Similar to most of the authors featured in *Ghost Writers*, Vonnegut struggled with his own personal demons. He had a disagreement with his wife, Jane, and moved to New York City in 1971. The two divorced but remained friends until her death in late 1986. Having lifelong issues with depression, he attempted suicide in 1984.

Vonnegut died on April 11, 2007, after a fatal fall in his New York City brownstone. The celebrated author had written fourteen novels, three short story collections, five plays, and five non-fiction books at the time of his death.

VONNEGUT'S HAUNT: VICTORIA HOUSE

PROVINCETOWN, MA—I spent the night at what turned out to be Provincetown's murder house. I was on assignment for a magazine and booked a weekend at the Victoria House on Standish Street. I was put into Room 4 and spent the night under my covers because I heard what sounded like muted cries or a whimper coming from a boarded-up closet. The following morning, I asked to be moved out of the spooky room. I intuitively knew something horrible had happened there.

Years later I found out that the Victoria House had a dark secret. Back in the 1960s, the B&B was a guest house and home to serial killer Tony "Chop Chop" Costa. He was convicted in 1970 of two of the four murders of the young women he allegedly slaughtered, including Patricia H. Walsh and Mary Ann Wysocki. The house, for a brief period, was often pointed out to tourists as the site where the murderer lived. Costa met his victims there before luring them to his "secret garden" of marijuana before murdering and mutilating them in Truro.

According to the July 25, 1969, article in *Life* magazine penned by *Slaughterhouse-Five* author Kurt Vonnegut, Costa's room at the Standish Street haunt was significant. "In his closet in the rooming house where he helped Patricia Walsh and Mary Ann Wysocki with their luggage, police found a coil of stained rope," Vonnegut wrote.

Guests at Provincetown's now closed Victoria House, located at 5 Standish Street, reported "uneasy feelings in the middle of the night accompanied with the smell of blood," Provincetown Paranormal Research Society posted. "Apparently it was once the home to a doctor or butcher?"

Victoria House was indeed the residence of the town's butcher, but one who cut up people, not livestock. His name was Tony Costa.

The Victoria House bed and breakfast's name is a bit misleading. "I thought the house was Victorian, thus the name. But it was a misnomer, as the house is definitely not Victorian," said the former owner who purchased it in 1972.

Every major city has one, a murder house. In Provincetown, it's located on Standish Street.

Costa's crimes were particularly gruesome. When the bodies were discovered, the hearts were supposedly missing, although this detail was later unsubstantiated. However, each corpse was crudely cut into parts. While the discovery of the victims caused a sensation, it was apparently the district attorney Edmund Dinis's description of the remains that caused the initial uproar. "The hearts of each girl had been removed from the bodies and were not in the graves, nor were they found," Dinis announced. "A razor like device was found near the graves. Each body was cut into as many parts as there are joints." Teeth marks were also found on the bodies.

When Vonnegut discussed the case in *Life* magazine on July 25, 1969, the story became a national sensation. "Jack the Ripper used to get compliments about the way he dissected the women he killed," wrote Vonnegut. "Now Cape Cod has a mutilator. The pieces of four young women were found in a shallow grave. Whoever did it was no artist with the knife. He chopped up the women with what the police guess was a brush hook or an ax. It couldn't have taken too long to do."

Vonnegut captured the vibe of Provincetown in this well-crafted story, mentioning telling observations including graffiti painted on a Truro laundromat: "Tony Costa digs girls."

He also poked fun at the thrill seekers. "When the bodies were found last winter, tourists arrived off-season," he wrote. "They wanted to help dig. They were puzzled when park rangers and police and firemen found them disgusting."

The story almost became the crime of the century. However, Charlie Manson's "Helter Skelter" murder spree in California trumped Costa's chopping frenzy. The "secret garden" killer was sentenced to life in prison and ended up committing suicide by hanging himself in his cell on May 12, 1974.

As far as hauntings are concerned, there have been reports of residual energy in Room 4. According to a former manager at the Victoria House, he would hear disembodied whispers throughout the guest house and the occasional scream of a female voice emanating from Room 4. Some believe that Costa may have kept his victims in the Victoria House, similar to what Buffalo Bill did in *Silence of the Lambs*, before murdering them, dismembering their corpses, and burying them in Truro.

"In the guest house on Standish Street, near the center of town, the slain girls checked in for a night last January," the *Life* piece explained. "At the time, Tony Costa was renting a room there by the week. He was introduced to the other guests by the landlady, Mrs. Patricia Morton."

The young women checked in but they never checked out.

RALPH WALDO EMERSON

Where's Waldo? If you're looking for the ghost of Ralph Waldo Emerson, the famous transcendentalist poet and lecturer, visit his old Ivy League stomping ground in Cambridge, Massachusetts. While he was born in Boston on May 25, 1803, and buried at Concord's Sleepy Hollow Cemetery in 1882, he spent his formative years as a starving student studying at Harvard Divinity School in the "City of Squares."

One of Emerson's old haunts on campus was the university's historic Wadsworth House, located at 1341 Massachusetts Avenue.

Built in 1726, this Early Georgian building is one of the few large houses not constructed by a Tory. Facing Massachusetts Avenue and an architectural anomaly of sorts thanks to its five-bay façade and simplistic Colonial design, Wadsworth House served as the primary residence for the president of Harvard until 1849. Over the years, the house would host visiting ministers and student boarders, including Emerson. The second-oldest surviving structure on Harvard's campus, the house lost its front yard when Massachusetts Avenue was widened.

Wadsworth House was also a major player in the days leading up to the Revolutionary War. The fight for independence began on April 19, 1775, and thousands of armed men from all over New England gathered in Cambridge. However, there was a housing shortage. Soldiers camped in the Cambridge Common while Harvard, responding to the growing anti-Tory sentiment and concerned about student safety, canceled classes on May 1 and allowed displaced soldiers to set up temporary shelter in its buildings.

On June 15, 1775, the Continental Congress appointed George Washington as commander in chief of the army, and he assumed his role as the leader of the troops on July 3, 1775. Washington set up his first headquarters at Wadsworth House and it's said that he hashed out plans to oust King George from Boston in the historic landmark's parlor room.

Washington, who remained in Cambridge until April 1776, later moved into his primary residence located at the Longfellow House on Brattle Street. Apparently, Wadsworth was in complete disrepair at the time.

In addition to its role in the Revolutionary War, Wadsworth House is also home to several reported Washington-era residual hauntings that continue to linger in the chambers of the colonial haunt. "One account explains that early one morning, forty years ago, a cleaning lady vacuuming alone in Wadsworth House saw a grim character in a tricorn hat and cloak silently come down the stairs and go out the door," reported the *Crimson* in 1997. The reporter, however, never confirmed the rumor, adding that "none of the staff at the Wadsworth House have heard anything about a man in a tricorn hat."

An article dating back to 1986 confirmed a similar story. "Over at Wadsworth House, where Washington once slept, ghosts of American Patriots wearing tricorn hats and cloaks have not haunted the colonial building in at least twenty-five years," the *Crimson* added.

Spirits wearing tricorn hats? Yep, Harvard Square allegedly has them. For the record, a residual haunting isn't technically a ghost but a playback or recording of a past event. Based on the so-called Stone Tape theory, apparitions aren't intelligent spirits that interact with the living, but psychic imprints that happen especially during moments of high tension, such as a murder or during intense moments of a person's life. According to the hypothesis, residual hauntings are simply non-interactive playbacks, similar to a movie.

Based on ghost lore, hauntings have been associated with the lack of proper burial or a later desecration of the grave. Countless spirits, according to paranormal researchers, have been traced to missing gravestones or vandalism of a resting place. In regard to the pre-Revolution spirit allegedly lingering in Wadsworth House, it's likely that the residual haunting is a psychic imprint of sorts associated with the intense military strategy sessions in the summer of 1775.

In November 1973, the senior editor of *Harvard Magazine*, with offices formerly located in the Wadsworth House, wrote an article called "The House Is Haunted and We Like It That Way," referring to the tricorn hat–wearing spirits allegedly haunting the almost three-hundred-year-old landmark. "For a society of rationalists, Harvardians are surprisingly interested in the supernatural," mused *Harvard Magazine*'s editor in 1998. "Clearly, all this talk about ghosts concerns Harvard's continuity and history and traditions—not séances and the ectoplasm."

Seriously? Based on reports from the cleaning lady who spotted the "grim character in a tricorn hat and cloak" levitating down the stairs, perhaps the ghosts of Harvard are more than a personification of the Ivy League's storied past. It's possible that the spirits of Wadsworth House are, in fact, ghostly reminders of the historically significant military sessions spearheaded by Washington in 1775.

EMERSON'S HAUNT: HARVARD YARD

CAMBRIDGE, MA—History and mystery lurk in just about every crimson corner of Cambridge's prestigious Ivy League. Harvard University is full of secrets, and its ghost lore reflects this centuries-old legacy of dead presidents and long-gone ghost writers. Spine-chilling tales of unexplained sounds, phantom knocking, and full-bodied apparitions have become a rite of passage for the uninitiated, college-bound progeny adapting to life in the Hogwarts-style halls scattered throughout Harvard Yard.

Elizabeth Tucker, a professor of English at Binghamton University and author of *Haunted Halls: Ghostlore of American College Campuses*, said that collegiate ghost stories are morality plays for the modern era. "They educate freshmen about how to live well in college," she explained in a 2007 interview, adding that the cautionary tales serve as spooky metaphors of fear, disorder, and insanity. They also reflect students' interest in their college's historical legacy. Campus ghost lore is a paranormal pep rally of sorts. "You don't find ghost stories at schools without a sense of pride," Tucker continued. "School spirits reflect school spirit."

The difference between Harvard's specters and other run-of-the-mill ghosts haunting universities throughout the country? Their spirits are wicked smart. Harvard's Massachusetts Hall has one respectable-looking student who returns every fall claiming to be a member of the class of 1914. Apparently, the residual apparition of Holbrook Smith never received the memo that he was kicked out of the Ivy League almost a century ago. There's also a Civil War–era apparition who allegedly haunts Memorial Hall. In 1929 a proctor reported seeing a man, who wasn't enrolled in the class, show up with a blue book in hand. The school spirit was known as the Memorial Hall ghost, and the "left behind" (a spirit who doesn't know he's dead) kept returning to class to finish the test—even though he died long ago.

In addition to Harvard's ghost lore, the university has secrets. However, not all of them are doom and gloom. For example, the iconic John Harvard statue positioned in front of the allegedly haunted University Hall. The Puritan-dressed model for the statue was Sherman Hore, a member of the class of 1882. After establishing the college in 1636, Harvard died in 1638, long before the statue was sculpted. So it's not actually the college's namesake depicted in the piece.

Tourists flock to the monument and believe rubbing his shiny foot will bring them good luck, kind of like the pilgrims who travel to St. Peter's Basilica in Rome to touch the foot of St. Peter. The difference between Harvard and St. Peter's, however, is that Harvard students reportedly urinate on the very foot that tourists rub. Heard of going to the John, right? Probably not how the Charlestown-based minister would like to be remembered.

Like the subterranean steam tunnels that connect the university's buildings, Harvard's darker mysteries are buried in the hard soil of Puritan thought. According to the *Crimson* in 1997, "In an institution with a past as long and as storied as Harvard's, one would expect at least a few ghost stories. Surprisingly, however, there is little on record."

The Yard is full of fearsome phantoms. They're just hiding. The ghosts of Harvard are lurking in the shadows, behind the historical buildings dotting the campus, and waiting for their stories to be told.

One such haunting involves Harvard's University Hall located in the center of the Yard. The white Chelmsford granite building, built between 1813 and 1815 by Harvard alum Charles Bulfinch, served as a massive first-floor dining hall known as the College Commons until it was partitioned into classrooms in 1849. The top floors boasted a chapel and library, but were later reconditioned for the Faculty of Arts and Sciences. Students and faculty who visited the hallowed structure claimed that if you listen closely near the building's southwest entrance, you can hear a riotous residual haunting from the past.

On November 1, 1818, students assembled for a peaceful Sunday dinner at University Hall. "Then all hell broke loose," wrote the *Harvard Gazette*. "A major food fight set off a cascade of disturbances, and within one week the entire sophomore class was expelled." It's known as the "Rebellion of 1818."

According to ghost lore, there were "sounds of a phantom dinner party that filled the corridor by the southwest corner of University Hall, a displaced echo of the dining hall that occupied the building in the nineteenth century," confirmed the *Crimson*. Apparently, the food fight was so over the top that it left a psychic imprint on the historic hall. It's what is known as a spirit-level recording, or residual haunting, that replays over and over again like a videotape. "How and why past events are recorded and replayed repetitiously is not understood," explained Lauren Forcella of the *Paranormal Network*. "Whatever the actual mechanism, it apparently possesses longevity, as the encore performances of a haunting can continue for decades or longer. Generally, the haunting is a fragment or portion of an actual event."

The College Commons dining hall was an open space, and reportedly the design "made it easy for students eventually to throw food, furniture and handy projectiles at rival classes. The adjoining chambers, wrote one contemporary, were like barrels of gunpowder stacked side by side." Someone threw a slice of buttered bread, which led to a full-blown food fight. Weapons of class destruction included teacups, plates and wood. The entire sophomore class, which included literary icon Ralph Waldo Emerson, was expelled after a series of protests and gatherings around what was known as the "protest tree." Of course, a majority of the eighty students, including Emerson, were reinstated.

The seeds of protest were firmly planted in the soil surrounding University Hall. In 1834 a group of freshmen found President Josiah Quincy III's iron fist enforcing rules unreasonable. So they torched a classroom, set off an explosion in Holden Chapel, and hanged Quincy in effigy— from the branches of the protest tree no doubt—which led to campus-wide revolt.

Many believe the rambunctious voices of protest continue to haunt Harvard's University Hall. However, some ghost lore experts claim the sounds from the phantom food fight disappeared in the late 1960s. Perhaps Harvard's Vietnam-era counterculture set the ghosts of the school's rebellious past free?

William C. "Burriss" Young, who lived in nearby Mass Hall as an assistant dean of freshmen and was known as a "veritable font of Harvard ghost lore," claimed that the spirited disembodied voices magically disappeared, pointing out that "no one has heard it since 'the bust.'" For the record, "the bust" referred to when students took over the hall in 1969 and occupied it for eighteen hours in protest of Harvard's stance on the Vietnam War. Massachusetts state police broke down the historic building's front doors to get in and remove the hippie troublemakers. Young said, "Since then, either the ghosts have been so distraught at the police breaking up the party or the breaking of the doors ruined something in the acoustics of the place, but no one's heard anything."

There's a quote by Emerson hidden behind the Yard's Meyer Gate confirming the university's school spirits: "Cambridge at any time is full of ghosts."

Perhaps he's right.

GHOST Q&A: CHRISTOPHER RONDINA

"The encounter left me curled on the floor, crying like a newborn. I was fifteen and my life changed that night."
— Christopher Rondina, *Legends of Sleepy Hollow*

Christopher Rondina, a paranormal-themed author and tour guide based in Newport, Rhode Island, digs deep for the skeletal secrets buried beneath New England's bloodstained soil. His latest book, *Legends of Sleepy Hollow: The Lost History of the Headless Horseman,* explores the real-life inspiration behind many of the characters featured in Washington Irving's classic, including the ghostly antagonist believed to be a Revolutionary War soldier.

"He was alleged to be a German mercenary working for the British Army, but his identity was unknown, even two hundred years later," Rondina told me. "I believed the answer to his mystery had to be out there somewhere, so I began digging, looking for any clues to the ghost's mortal existence. The answer was out there, but I had to go to Germany to find it, hidden among centuries-old military records."

In the interview, Rondina doesn't "give up the ghost" but he talked candidly about his spirited journey of becoming the go-to

PHOTO COURTESY CHRISTOPHER RONDINA.

author focusing on New England's vampires, Irving's headless horseman, and the North Atlantic's ghost pirates. Argh, matey!

Q: How did you get your start as an author of paranormal-themed books?
A: I never aspired to be a writer. My original plan was to be an illustrator. In fact, it was illustrating that led me to write my first book. I'd grown up loving Halloween, monsters, and ghost stories so I was blessed to live in New England where we take so much pride in our rich haunted history.

As a teenager I became fascinated by New England's strange tradition of believing in vampires, which was not well known at the time. I started to collect anything I could on the subject, and by my late twenties I'd accumulated an impressive folio of newspaper clippings and documents connected to vampire folklore in early America. A friend encouraged me to publish my collection like a scrapbook alongside my own illustrations, and it seemed like a great idea to me.

Unfortunately, it quickly became clear that a book of random newspaper clippings without any context wasn't going to appeal to anyone. With a bit of nudging I wrote a preface, and then brief introductions to each article, but it still felt very incomplete. I expanded, edited, filled in the gaps, and over several months I began to realize I was writing chapters around each newspaper clipping. In essence, I wrote my first book without realizing I was doing it.

By some miracle, the early manuscript was picked up by a publisher on Cape Cod in 1996, and eventually became my book *Vampires of New England.*

Q: How has your experience as a tour guide shaped you as an author?
A: The connection between my work as a storyteller and my writing is symbiotic. I'd done very little public speaking before my first book was released. Afterward, I was in demand at schools and events to talk about vampires and the paranormal. I enjoyed creating presentations, but I felt like a podium and microphone weren't the ideal format for these stories.

By sheer chance, a day trip to Sleepy Hollow in October of 1997 became the catalyst that would change my career forever. While visiting the village's Old Dutch Church I met an elderly caretaker who looked like Rip Van Winkle. He told me stories about the famous characters buried in the churchyard and their connections to the village's most famous legend. The joy he took in relating the burial ground's history was wonderful to see. I decided that I wanted to follow his example, to get my stories out of the classroom and into the world. Yes, a graveyard walk was the perfect venue.

Twenty years later, I'm still storytelling whether it's in graveyards, on the ocean, or along the historic streets of my colonial hometown.

Q: What are some of your favorite haunted locations in Rhode Island and why?
A: Rhode Island is a small state, but it's got more than a fair share of ghost stories, haunted sites, and supernatural legends. One of my favorites is Fort Adams, where a nineteenth-century soldier was murdered on the Fourth of July and is still alleged to throw rocks at trespassers in the old tunnels.

My top pick, however, has to be Newport's Long Wharf, where pirates were hanged in the eighteenth century. It's one of the oldest wharves in the city, and it's directly across from a small harbor island where criminals were once buried. After the capture of the pirate ship *Ranger* in the early 1720s, the crew members were tried and sentenced to hang. Gallows were built at the far end of the wharf near the harbor entrance for all to see, and the bodies were left hanging for months as a gruesome warning to other pirates who might try to make port in the town.

When the pirates were eventually cut down, their bodies were rowed over to the barren, unhallowed ground of Goat Island and buried in shallow graves at the water's edge. High tide covered the burials, low tide left them exposed, so they were buried 'neither on land nor at sea' to curse their souls to endless unrest.

Locals still claim to hear the men of the *Ranger* whispering from the water's edge on moonless nights. The story is so mythic, so cinematic, yet it's based on real and documented history. It doesn't get any cooler than ghost pirates.

Q: What inspired you to write *Legends of Sleepy Hollow: The Lost History of the Headless Horseman*?
A: I've loved Washington Irving's *Legend of Sleepy Hollow* since I was a boy. I didn't learn it was a real place until my early twenties, but afterward I made a point to visit the village whenever I could. I discovered that Irving's story was inspired by genuine local people and places, and even the legendary ghost was taken from the folklore of the old Dutch families of the region.

The idea of publishing an edition of the original story alongside the real history was bouncing around in my head for years, but when the two-hundredth anniversary came around I knew the time was right to finally make it happen.

Q: What are your thoughts on ghosts and any memorable first-hand encounters?
A: I'm a skeptical believer, if that makes any sense. To be honest, it doesn't always make sense to me. I've encountered quite a lot of phenomena, seen a lot of evidence, but it's not often I see something that can't be explained in perfectly ordinary terms. However, there have been a few incidents that seemed decidedly unearthly.

The most striking was my own first experience with a ghost almost forty years ago. A figure appeared in my room, which was a bedroom in an 1870s Victorian house in my hometown of Newport, Rhode Island. She clearly had something she needed to say, and did her best to communicate with me. But all I could feel from her was a deep, overwhelming sorrow.

The encounter left me curled on the floor, crying like a newborn. I was fifteen, and my life changed that night. No matter how many hoaxes, false alarms, or fruitless investigations I've experienced . . . I will always believe.

Q: Anything else?
A: *Legends of Sleepy Hollow* was a true labor of love for me, an opportunity to pay homage to America's first great ghost story. Over the last twenty years I've had the privilege to explore countless iconic hauntings across the Northeast. In *Vampires of New England*, I chronicle dozens of graveyards supposedly haunted by malevolent undead creatures and even connect our local bloodsuckers to the legend of Dracula.

My family's nautical heritage inspired me to write *Ghost Ships of New England*, which explores phantom schooners, lost ships, haunted lighthouses, and pirate folklore all along the North Atlantic coast.

Grim and ghoulish stories like the murderous tale of Lizzie Borden and the dark history of Salem Village are at the heart of my book *Ghosts of New England*, along with a spirit-infested castle, vengeful witches, Yankee werewolves, cursed apples, and even a newly unearthed vampire grave.

THE BELIEVERS

"It was like some dark undefinable menace, forever dogging my steps, lurking, and threatening."
—EDITH WHARTON, *THE GHOST STORIES OF EDITH WHARTON*

GHOST PROFILE: ROBERT OAKES

"Wharton saw a creative opportunity in exploring her own fear of ghosts, which, apparently, she felt from the time she was a girl."
—Robert Oakes, *The Mount Tour Guide*

Robert Oakes, tour guide at Edith Wharton's The Mount in Lenox, Massachusetts, lit up when I mentioned I was an author on assignment for a paranormal-themed travel book. "You should definitely go on one of my ghost tours," he said after guiding me through the history and mystery behind Wharton's breathtakingly picturesque Berkshires estate. "I'm also working on a book about the hauntings in the area."

When I'm not writing my historical-based ghost books, I give tours at historic house museums such as the Turner-Ingersoll Mansion named after Nathaniel Hawthorne's gothic novel, *The House of the Seven Gables.* I identified with Oakes's enthusiasm. There's something magical about giving tours at a place as architecturally significant as The Mount . . . bonus points if the location is paranormally active.

Wharton's estate is extremely haunted.

"I once had that 'tingles-on-the-neck' sensation of something unseen following close behind me during a tour," Oakes told me. "I

PHOTO COURTESY ROBERT OAKES

also once heard what sounded like a voice speaking my name close to my ear. But when I looked around, I saw no one else with me on the floor."

According to him, Wharton's former home is teeming with spirits from the mansion's gilded-age past. He signed on as a house guide in 2009 and soon started giving night tours to accommodate the growing interest in the ghost lore associated with Wharton's country estate thanks to two investigations featured on Syfy's *Ghost Hunters* in 2009 and 2015.

Oakes said the team from The Atlantic Paranormal Society (TAPS) definitely stirred the pot of both interest and paranormal activity. "I would say their visits certainly helped stir up interest in our ghosts," he said. "Their first investigation took place the same year The Mount began offering the ghost tour, and there was a great deal of enthusiasm right from the start, partly fueled by the interest of the *Ghost Hunters*. The tours themselves then began to yield new stories, as people began reporting things they said happened to them while on a ghost tour, and our ghostly reputation grew and grew."

When *Ghost Hunters* investigated The Mount in 2015, Oakes was featured in the historic house museum's press release. "It was fantastic to welcome Jason, Steve, Tango and the rest of the *Ghost Hunters* team back to The Mount for a second investigation," he said in the release. "There have been so many reports of strange activity at the estate since their last visit, it isn't surprising they wanted to return."

In 2015, Oakes was the only staff member at The Mount allowed to work directly with the TAPS team. "I was there during the second investigation with the *Ghost Hunters* and I do remember a kind of electric feeling in the air, particularly on the bedroom floor of the main house, immediately after they wrapped for the night," he recalled. "It felt to me like the ghosts were a bit agitated."

In the release, Oakes identified the paranormal hot spots at The Mount including "the second floor of the historic stable, Wharton's bathroom on the second floor of the main house and Teddy Wharton's den on the first floor. Footsteps, strange sensations, the distinct scents of floral perfume and cigar smoke have all been reported by guests."

When I asked if the locations he cited in the press release are still the estate's most haunted, Oakes nodded. "The most active location is the second floor of the stable," he told me. "It's one of the few remaining unrestored areas of the estate, so that certainly helps to give it the right feel. But more than that, there is a strong sense that spirits linger there. At the very top of the building, you can dimly see a storage area through a darkened doorway in the hayloft. One of our scariest encounters is said to have happened in there. There's a hallway that opens to a number of rooms where people have reported seeing strange shadows moving around."

Oakes said that Wharton penned several ghost stories during her career, and pulled from her personal experiences with the paranormal. When she was a girl, Wharton claimed to be "haunted by formless horrors" and was terrified of shadow figures until her late twenties. Oakes said the *Age of Innocence* writer became more comfortable with the spooky subject matter while living at The Mount and would pen a collection of her own ghost stories later in life.

"Wharton wrote in her autobiography of a 'dark undefinable menace' that she felt was 'forever dogging [her] footsteps.' Over the years, there have been many reports at The Mount of a dark, featureless shadow figure seen in hallways, in rooms, even on walls," Oakes explained. "It's possible these phenomena are connected, but who can say for sure?"

When asked why he thought the author was so haunted by the ghosts of her childhood, Oakes said it could be related to Wharton's bout with typhoid fever when she was only nine years old. She contracted the illness during a family vacation in the Black Forest of Germany.

"There may be a connection between a near-fatal illness that she experienced as a child and the onset of these paranormal fears," he said. "I don't know for sure whether the illness inspired the fears, but it did seem to affect her deeply."

Oakes believes that the ghost stories were the *Ethan Frome* author's way of facing her fears. "Wharton saw a creative opportunity in exploring her own fear of ghosts, which, apparently, she felt from the time she was a girl," he told me. "I imagine she felt her own visceral reactions were fertile ground for good writing."

In addition to the shadow figure spotted throughout The Mount, Oakes said he has seen photos of what looks like a ghostly woman with sad, sunken eyes peering from the third-floor bathroom window. "It's hard to say who that might be, though I was told by the woman who sent us the photograph [that she] had an intuition that the spirit's name was Anna, which was the name of Wharton's governess," Oakes said.

As far as other locations at The Mount that give Oakes the creeps, he said Wharton's pet cemetery has a spooky aesthetic that serves as the perfect backdrop to his evening ghost tours. "While I don't know of any encounters in the pet cemetery, I will say that the wind can sometimes whip up very suddenly as we stand out there during the tour," he said. "And there was one night when we heard the sound of wolves howling in the distance. That certainly helped set the mood."

Oakes, currently working on his first collection of ghost stories for the History Press, said there are several hot spots in the Lenox area that are popular among paranormal investigators. "There are many reportedly haunted places in the Berkshires," he continued. "One of the most well-known is the Hoosac Tunnel, also known as 'the bloody pit,' which has inspired ghost stories since it was first built in the 1800s."

Michael Norman and Beth Scott wrote about the ghost lore associated with the so-called "bloody pit" in *Historic Haunted America*. "The digging of this railroad tunnel is a saga of blood,

The Mount is a country estate in Lenox, Massachusetts, and was the home of noted American author Edith Wharton. PHOTO COURTESY DEPOSIT PHOTOS.

sweat and tears. Begun in 1851, it wasn't finished until 1875. During those twenty-four years, hundreds of miners, using mostly crude black powder and pick and shovel, chipped away at the unyielding rock of Hoosac Mountain," Norman and Scott wrote. "By the time the tunnel was finished, two hundred men had lost their lives in what came to be known as 'the bloody pit.' Most died in explosions, fires, and drownings, but one death may not have been accidental."

Two men, Ned Brinkman and Billy Nash, were killed during a nitroglycerin-induced explosion on March 20, 1865. The man who prematurely set off the explosion, Ringo Kelley, managed to escape the wrath of "the bloody pit" that afternoon, but one year later he mysteriously disappeared. Kelley's body was found two miles inside the Hoosac Tunnel, at the exact spot where Brinkman and Nash had died. He'd been strangled to death. There were no suspects . . . at least among the living.

How did Kelley die? Ghost lore enthusiasts claimed that he was murdered by the vengeful spirits of Brinkman and Nash. Over the years, multiple sources who were brave enough to venture inside the Hoosac Tunnel claimed to see phantom miners and hear mysterious groans.

One man, Frank Webster, said he was summoned inside "the bloody pit" in 1874 by a voice in the darkness. Webster then said he saw floating apparitions. One of the apparitions supposedly grabbed Webster's rifle and hit him over the head with it. He was missing for three days and later told authorities about his close encounter in the tunnel. According to the police report, when Webster showed up, his rifle was missing and he looked like he'd seen a ghost.

While the extremely haunted Houghton Mansion in North Adams was recently purchased and closed to paranormal investigators, Oakes recommended Ventfort Hall, also in Lenox, which has been investigated by the *Ghost Hunters* and other paranormal teams.

Oakes said he enjoys turning people on to Wharton's legacy as well as the house she designed and loved on his tours. "Many people don't know that Wharton, herself, was a writer of ghost stories and loved a good, scary tale,", he told *The Berkshire Eagle* on November 17, 2015. "In sharing our own stories, as we appeal to the imagination and a sense of mystery, I feel we are honoring her work and passion."

EDITH WHARTON

Did Edith Wharton suffer from a lifelong spirit attachment, or was it something psychosomatic? In her autobiography *A Backward Glance*, she wrote about a "dark undefinable menace" that seemed to follow her for decades. The featureless figure that haunted her until her death on August 11, 1937, continues to lurk in the shadows of The Mount, Wharton's later-in-life home in Lenox, Massachusetts.

The American novelist, who won a Pulitzer Prize for *The Age of Innocence*, had a laundry list of phobias that probably seemed irrational to the average person. She was afraid of animals except for the small furry dogs that she treated like her children. In fact, she had a pet cemetery for her beloved puppies on her estate and she would gaze from her bedroom window at their final resting spot.

Wharton would have debilitating panic attacks when she visited her family. She had an irrational fear that a crone would open the door at her parent's home. She also strongly disliked supernatural-themed stories, especially fairy tales featuring women with magical powers. Wicked witches and evil stepmothers mortified her on a deep, visceral level. Wharton couldn't even sleep in a room that contained a book of ghost stories until her late twenties.

The famed author was born into New York's aristocracy. The phrase, "Keeping up with the Joneses?" describes her family. Wharton's father, George Frederic Jones, made his money from real estate during the Gilded Age and she lived in New York City and Newport, Rhode Island, most of her childhood. Wharton's relationship with her mother, Lucretia, was strained and it's believed that her neuroses were exacerbated by strict parenting.

She suffered from post-traumatic stress disorder (PTSD) from a near-fatal bout with typhoid fever during a family vacation in Germany's Black Forest. Wharton was only nine years old when she was stricken with the illness. She was quarantined in the German hospital and was completely cut off from visitors, including her parents. Wharton's only human contact was the white-robed doctor who treated her. The physician would hover in the doorway, rather than entering her hospital room, to avoid the contagion.

Based on a psychological analysis from Lenor C. Terr's book called *Childhood Trauma and the Creative Product*, Wharton possibly replayed the trauma over and over throughout her life. Could this traumatic childhood image be the source of the shadow figure that haunted Wharton? Terr believes the doctor-in-the-doorway scene was responsible for her irrational fear of thresholds. The psychologist also argued that the forced isolation in the Black Forest was at the heart of Wharton's ghost stories—such as "All Souls," which featured a bedridden protagonist—and continued to traumatize her into adulthood.

In other words, the only ghosts that existed in Wharton's world were the ones that lived inside her head.

But that doesn't explain the shadow-figure manifestations seen not only by Wharton herself, but spotted by visitors at The Mount in the Berkshires. Could it be a "thought-form" or "tulpa" haunting the author's estate in Lenox? A thought-form entity is created by the human mind and given energy from an individual or group of people. It's not a spirit in the traditional sense, but a projection of the concentrated thoughts of living people.

I reached out to my friends in the paranormal community and they strongly believe that human-created entities are possible. "Thought-forms are real energy," explained Barbara Williams, a psychic-medium based in Maine. Ken DeCosta, a respected paranormal researcher and founder of Riseup Paranormal Society in Rhode Island, agreed with Williams. "Once any thought is fully formed, it becomes something tangible," he told me, adding that he's experienced thought-forms out in the field and was able to measure them.

Could the entity lurking in the shadows of The Mount be a "thought-form" created by Wharton's deepest, darkest fears? It's possible.

WHARTON'S HAUNT: THE MOUNT

LENOX, MA—It felt as if we were being transported back in time when my friend Andrew Warburton and I pulled into the labyrinthine driveway leading up to Edith Wharton's The Mount. I was psychically drawn to the Georgian Revival gatehouse and stable near the entrance, but I was unable to check it out because it was locked during the winter months.

There was an inexplicable, "something wicked this way comes" vibe as we entered the estate's promenade hidden behind a series of well-manicured pleached linden trees. Wharton strongly viewed her gardens as a series of outdoor rooms, living in harmony with the house's white-stucco exterior accented with dark green shutters and juxtaposed with the Berkshire's rustic landscape.

Mission accomplished.

However, as we inched closer to the turn-of-the-century house museum that Wharton lovingly called her "first real home," it felt like we were being watched. Wharton wrote about being "haunted by formless horrors." Were the shadows from *The Age of Innocence* author's past peering at us from the third-floor window?

Wharton and her husband Edward (Teddy) lived in The Mount from 1902 to 1911. After the couple left, the house became a private residence, a girls' dormitory for the Foxhollow School, and home of the theatre company Shakespeare & Company. It was during its tenure as a dormitory and Shakespearean performance space that the ghost sightings seemed to surface. The theatre group's resident actors reported unexplained sounds and ghostly figures wearing period dress.

In 2009 the team from SyFy's *Ghost Hunters* checked out the property and followed it up with a second visit in 2015. During the initial three-day investigation, The Atlantic Paranormal Society, better known as TAPS, captured audio and video evidence suggesting paranormal activity, which included phantom footsteps in empty rooms and disembodied voices.

Ghost Hunters returned to The Mount six years later after employees at the museum claimed an increase in activity, including the appearance of two full-bodied apparitions sitting in the drawing room. "The figures, a man and a woman, are reported to be reading in silence in a spot where

Wharton and her husband, Teddy, were known to recline," wrote Jennifer Huberdeau in *The Berkshire Eagle* on November 17, 2015.

In the article called "*Ghost Hunters* to air new episode filmed at The Mount in Lenox," Steve Gonsalves from TAPS talked about several pieces of evidence, including a thermal image of a large handprint that left the paranormal team with more questions than answers when they investigated the property in 2009. "The older the building, the greater possibility that the structure will have seen some trauma, such as family deaths and murder," Gonsalves told *The Eagle* via email. "It's not always connected to the structure though; it could be connected to an object or even the land."

There was a rumor that a servant hanged herself in the cupola of the mansion after she learned she was pregnant. Not true. The legend was debunked by the TAPS team.

However they did pick up high-frequency readings on the K2 meter when the *Ghost Hunters* investigated the attic. Also, a "black box" device made a loud shriek during an EVP session in the building's top floor and two crew members heard phantom footsteps running away from them and down the steps.

In the 2015 episode, the *Ghost Hunters* revisited the mansion and talked with tour guide Robert Oakes. "When I first started working here at The Mount, I was a skeptic," Oakes told TAPS. "But I've heard so many stories from visitors and staff members. I've had unusual experiences, which certainly leads me to believe that something strange is going on here at The Mount," Oakes said. "I was in the drawing room and there was no one around and I heard what sounded like my name spoken in my ear. That was a strange experience."

Oakes said he's heard reports of shadow figures throughout the house, especially near the Henry James guest room on the third floor. "I had a co-worker with me and she was running a broom over the floor," reported Lisa Pixley, a former housekeeper. "One of the floorboards had come up and at the point a black figure floated by. We both saw it and we were both freaked out. It was very scary."

Also on the third floor, another woman from the cleaning crew claimed to have seen a shadow figure that was approximately seven feet tall peering at her from the doorway and then leaned back in. Terrified, the housekeeper fled the house and never returned.

Oakes told *Ghost Hunters* that activity had spiked since the first visit in 2009. "More and more people are coming forward with stories with things that they've experienced here," he explained. "The number of stories keeps growing and growing. Some believe that it's Edith Wharton at The Mount. However, many people seem to think it's Teddy Wharton's presence still lingering in the house."

The Mount is where the Wharton's marriage began to unravel. Teddy Wharton's bouts with depression and the fact that he embezzled Edith's trust fund took a toll on the couple's relationship. They sold the estate in 1911 and then got a divorce.

What did the TAPS team find during the 2015 investigation? They picked up a female voice on the third floor and a weird figure appeared in the thermal camera near the Henry James guest room. The evidence, which included the sounds of a doors opening and closing, supported the first-hand anecdotes and suggested that the ghosts lingering on the third floor of the mansion aren't intelligent but residual, so it's like a videotaped loop playing over and over.

HENRY WADSWORTH LONGFELLOW

Henry Wadsworth Longfellow, the American literary icon and professor famous for his rhythmic cadences in poems such as "Paul Revere's Ride" and "The Village Blacksmith," moved to Cambridge in 1854 and set up home in the so-called haunted house where he both lived and died. Longfellow set up shop at the mid-Georgian mansion, known as the Vassall-Craigie-Longfellow House and built in 1759 by Major John Vassall, a wealthy Tory Row Loyalist.

Before Longfellow, George Washington lived there for ten months between July 1775 and April 1776 and used the building as his headquarters when he was leading the newly formed Continental army. For the record, Washington planned the Siege of Boston from the Tory Row house, and according to Hugh Howard's *Houses of the Founding Fathers*, Washington found the stellar view of the Charles River particularly useful. His maneuvering resulted in the evacuation of thousands of British soldiers and Loyalists back to England.

It's that view that initially attracted Longfellow to the historic Brattle Street estate. Elizabeth Craigie owned the house in the early 1800s and rented rooms out to Harvard students. Longfellow became one of Craigie's lodgers in 1837 and had a close encounter with a full-bodied apparition of what he believed was America's founding father. In April 1840, Longfellow watched the gardener's house catch fire and burn down. Locals gathered to put out the blaze, and Longfellow noticed something odd emerge from the smoke. "In the midst of it all, I saw slowly riding under the elms on the green in front of the house, a figure on horseback," he wrote in a letter. "It seemed like the ghost of Washington, directing the battle."

Longfellow's first wife, Mary Potter, died in 1835 following a miscarriage. He soon began courting Frances "Fanny" Appleton, the daughter of a wealthy Boston industrialist. He would walk over the Boston Bridge from Cambridge to the Appletons' home in Beacon Hill. In 1906, the bridge was renamed the Longfellow Bridge in honor of the late great poet.

After seven years of courting and dealing with "periods of neurotic depression," Longfellow received a letter from Appleton that would temporarily quell his anxiety. On May 10, 1843, Appleton agreed to marry Longfellow, and as a wedding gift from his wife's father, the two moved into the historic Vassall-Craigie House. Longfellow fathered six children with Appleton.

According to lore, their Tory Row estate was teeming with spirits. "The story that this house is haunted has been current for several generations," wrote Dorothy Dudley in *Theatrum Majorum* in 1875. Longfellow, skeptical of the ghost lore, would muse about an encounter he had coming home one night from the Dante Club. "When he crossed the garden he was startled by a white figure swaying before him," remembered William Dean Howells in *The White Mr. Longfellow*. "But he knew that the only way was to advance upon it. He pushed boldly forward and was suddenly caught under the throat—by the clothesline—with a long nightgown on it." In other words, Longfellow had a logical explanation to debunk all the conjecture surrounding the spirits inhabiting his house.

It was all hocus pocus. Or was it?

His wife, however, was more of a believer. In fact, Fanny's brother Tom Appleton was interested in the Spiritualism movement and introduced a well-known intuitive, Alice Goodrich, to the Longfellows. Goodrich, whom Appleton described as a "very strong medium," would allegedly channel the spirits and write cryptic messages from the dead, known as "automatic writing," that could be deciphered when held up to a mirror. Goodrich wrote one of her spirit letters to Longfellow, a benevolent message that ends with "let us drink."

Unfortunately Goodrich's so-called psychic abilities couldn't predict the horrors Longfellow would experience at home. On July 9, 1861, his wife was in the library reportedly sealing locks of their children's hair with a lit candle and envelopes. Somehow the wax—or, as in one theory suggested by their daughter, Allegra, a lit match—caught her summer dress on fire, and it was quickly engulfed in flames. Longfellow was taking a nap and after he was awakened by a loud scream rushed in to throw a rug around his wife, but it was too late to save her. Appleton died the following morning at 10:00 a.m.

The poet was injured by the blaze and unable to attend her funeral. According to reports, he grew his trademark beard to cover up the scars from the tragedy. However, his emotional scars lingered. "Everywhere he walked in the house, he told me later, he saw mother," wrote E. Ashley Rooney in *Cambridge, Massachusetts: Ghosts, Legends & Lore*, paraphrasing their daughter's diary. "She was in the library knitting, in the study talking and laughing with him, in the parlor dancing with us."

Coincidentally, Fanny's funeral was held on what would have been the couple's eighteenth wedding anniversary. "Frances was laid on a table in the center covered with flowers including white roses," wrote Rob Velella in his *Haunted Houses* tour. "She also had a wreath of orange blossoms around her head."

After his wife's death, Longfellow was tormented by the real-life horror he had witnessed in the library. According to his daughter's recollections, as told to Rooney, he had late-night conversations with the ghost of his dead wife and would dance with her apparition. "I think that ultimately he believed that she was there and because he believed, we believed," Rooney wrote. "Her spirit hovered over us."

Longfellow turned to laudanum and ether to self-medicate and begged "not to be sent to an asylum." The poet, who took a break from writing, said he was "inwardly bleeding to death." His heart was broken.

On September 21, 1865, Longfellow was mysteriously visited by one of the Fox sisters, major players in the Spiritualism movement, who allegedly interacted with the spirit world in the form of mysterious rapping sounds, or what Longfellow called "spiritual manifestations." The grieving poet invited Kate Fox into the library, the scene of his wife's death, and he heard a series of phantom rappings, which included "knocks on the door, on the table, on the floor," he recalled in a letter.

Longfellow died in 1882 and was buried next to his wife in Mount Auburn Cemetery.

Is the Longfellow House haunted? People who have toured the mansion have seen a lady in white, wearing period costume in the bedroom upstairs. Laura West, an intuitive at Divine Lotus Healing, said she's heard of people being "touched in specific spots in the house," she wrote online. She also learned about the lady in white from the Longfellow House guide. "Once or twice, she's heard other tour guides tell stories about people on the tours, asking 'who was that actress upstairs sitting on the bed? Her clothing looked so authentic.' Only to discover that the staff doesn't employ actors in period costume."

Longfellow's own poem "Haunted Houses" oddly answers the is-it-or-isn't-it question: "All houses wherein men have lived and died are haunted houses," he wrote. "Through the open doors the harmless phantoms on their errands glide with feet that make no sound upon the floors."

LONGFELLOW'S HAUNT: WAYSIDE INN

SUDBURY, MA—Jerusha Howe, the resident wailing spirit of Longfellow's Wayside Inn, was known as the Belle of Sudbury. She's also said to have died in 1842 from a broken heart. Her legend, which was immortalized by the paranormal investigation team from the Travel Channel's *Ghost Adventures*, has morphed over the years.

However, one story has been consistent. The ghostly woman is said to haunt both Room 9, her old bed chamber, and Room 10, which is believed to be where she sewed.

Longfellow's Wayside Inn was built in 1716. Originally called Howe Tavern, it was renamed after Henry Wadsworth Longfellow visited the historic hotspot with his publisher James Fields in October 1862. Longfellow penned the book *Tales of a Wayside Inn* in 1863.

Jerusha was the oldest sister of the last Howe innkeeper, Lyman, who was known as "the squire" back in the 1800s. "She was well educated, well dressed and loved to paint and read and sing to the guests and visitors of the inn," explained former innkeeper John Cowden to WBZ-TV. "People want this room because of the history with Jerusha. Its ambiance, dark paneling and plank flooring," the innkeeper explained, adding that there's a Secret Drawer Society allowing guests to leave notes of what they experienced in Room 9.

According to Cowden, guests claim they hear Howe playing her piano and walking around in the night. The innkeeper told WBZ-TV that he's never encountered the ghosts of Longfellow's Wayside Inn. "I have not experienced them myself, but because we heard so many, you just don't know," he continued.

The man who ditched Howe promised to come back to Sudbury to continue their courtship, but he never did. Born in 1797, she died at forty-five, unmarried and heartbroken.

What happened to her beloved? "Little is known of Jerusha's romantic affairs in life, but as the story goes, she was engaged to an Englishman," explained Alyson Horrocks in *Yankee magazine*. "The legend claims that he sailed home to England to make arrangements for the wedding and was never heard from again. There has been speculation that he drowned at sea, or he simply abandoned her, and perhaps he never existed at all."

According to *Ghost Adventures* front man Zak Bagans, Jerusha is "America's most amorous female ghost," and he felt her spirit was teasing him during the paranormal investigation or "lockdown," making Bagans want more.

"Longfellow's Wayside Inn is home to America's most romantic haunt," announced Bagans on the February 2011 Travel Channel episode. "The ghost of a woman who still pines away waiting for her lover to return from across the sea is experienced throughout the building. It is said that she only focuses on the men who sleep in her bedroom."

In the episode, Bagans continued to sexualize the dead woman's postmortem pleas for the British visitor she fell in love with in the early 1840s. He jokingly surmised that "guests have had intimate encounters with Jerusha" and announced his intentions to "hook up" with the female spirit at Longfellow's Wayside Inn. "Sorry everybody to bug your Valentine's Day dinner," Bagans awkwardly said from the dinner table. "I do have something I would like to say. There's a spirit of a woman who is very beautiful. She's gorgeous, and that's who I'm going to hook up with."

Bagans interviewed Dan Grillo, a regular overnight guest who stays in the notoriously haunted Room 9. Grillo said he had a face-to-face encounter with Jerusha's ghost, adding that "it wasn't sexual. It was comforting." The spirit allegedly only appears to men, even when the man's wife is sharing the bed.

"It was two in the morning," recalled Grillo. "An arm went around me and went across my back, and I was like, 'who is this?' I jumped up at the side of the bed. It was a clear impression."

Was it Jerusha? "Oh yeah," Grillo responded. "Other people I've talked to say they've seen her standing in the corner."

Bagan's investigation produced some compelling evidence. He claimed to have seen a ghostly dress sway near Jerusha's room, although it wasn't captured on camera. The team did film a misty form with a distinct head using a full-spectrum camera. They also experienced female cries, mysterious tapping, temperature fluctuations, and doors slamming in both Room 9 and 10. Bagans claimed Jerusha put her icy-cold hands on his knees and that the spirit played with his belt. After the lockdown, Bagans spent a night alone in Howe's room to get to know her better. Fellow cast mates Nick Groff and Aaron Goodwin joked that Bagans had a "ghost fetish."

Based purely on the special Valentine's Day *Ghost Adventures* episode, Howe is a sex-crazed succubus. Michael Baker, founder of the scientific group called the New England Center for the Advancement of Paranormal Science (NECAPS) and lead investigator with Para-Boston, said Bagans painted an over-the-top and somewhat misogynistic portrait of Wayside Inn's resident ghost.

Howe is heartbroken over an unrequited love affair. Based on Baker's exhaustive research, she possibly left a psychic imprint from her emotional breakdown when the Englishman didn't respond to her letters.

Apparently, the cliché "hell hath no fury like a woman scorned" also applies in the afterlife.

"That *Ghost Adventures* episode is horrendous," responded Baker. "We have captured a lot of evidence at the Wayside Inn over the years. It started with a knock on the door. The entire group heard it and looked at the door, and we recorded it. We opened the door right away, and no one was there. The stairs outside are narrow, curved and extremely creaky. No one could have knocked on that door and got away that fast unheard."

Baker's "real science, real answers" mantra cuts through the usual smoke and mirrors associated with the "Boo!" business. With Baker, there's no over-the-top *Ghostbusters* gear or fake Cockney accents. When it comes to science-based paranormal investigations, Baker is the real deal.

"Basically, there is no ghost-catching device," explained Baker. "The field has changed. It has taken more of a funhouse approach—it has become a novelty—and it has set the paranormal investigation field back in a way. A lot of people are trying to use a screwdriver to hammer a nail. People go in with preconceived notions, and if anything happens, they're going to come to a certain conclusion. If something moves, bumps or they hear footsteps, they're going to automatically assume that it's a ghost, and that's a bad way to investigate."

Baker continued, "Technology can't detect spirits . . . We have to prove that spirits exist before we can build anything that can measure them. There was a shift in the field, occurring in the nineties, where it [became] a game to mimic what is seen on television. There was a period where it was purely scientific, and now people think they can turn off the lights, pick up an infrared camera, and capture a ghost."

Baker said Longfellow's Wayside Inn is arguably the most active location he's investigated. "We recorded a video of a shadow coming out of the floor twice. The first time it came out of the floor and back down, and the next time it flew over the bed. This video confirmed the location of guest sightings. Then I recorded someone fumbling on a piano at 4:00 a.m. It wasn't a song. It was fumbling, and it lasted twenty minutes. Jerusha's piano is there, but it doesn't work and is in the museum at the other end of the inn. It was audible to the ears, and I couldn't hear it outside the room. Jerusha used to play that piano in her room."

The paranormal investigator said Howe's cries were captured on tape. "We recorded crying on a device that only records electromagnetic fields. It was captured in the same area as the shadow. It blew our mind because it was someone bawling," he explained.

"That same night, the hot water in the bathroom turned on by itself. We had cameras running in the room while we ate dinner. When we returned from dinner, the water in the bathroom had turned on. We could hear the water running on our recordings. We listened to the recordings when the last person used the bathroom, and no water was heard. So, something turned the water on full blast while we left the room. The bathroom is also in the same area as the shadow."

Baker, who's normally Para-Boston's skeptic, said he believes that Longfellow's Wayside Inn is one of the most haunted locations in Massachusetts. "I'm convinced because each time these things occurred, they happened with strict controls and monitoring of the environment," Baker continued. "There was no obvious explanation, and these things should not have been possible. They shouldn't have occurred, but they did."

The paranormal investigator said the Wayside Inn's ghost lore extends beyond Jerusha. "There was a sighting at the end of the 1800s of a half-body woman walking through what is now the ballroom. It left such an impression that they renamed the room the Hobgoblin Room.

According to Brian E. Plumb's *A History of Longfellow's Wayside Inn*, "[A] woman of the Howe family [long ago] claimed she saw a ghost floating, half running through this room on a dark night." The Hobgoblin Room, once called the Old Hall, was rechristened in 1868 after the historic ghost sighting.

Baker and his team have spent months scanning and transcribing letters from the Secret Drawer Society, which chronicle guests' encounters with Howe's ghost. A tradition dating to 1990 but believed to have started in 1923, the notes are kept in the nooks and crannies of Jerusha's room. "The best part about them is its unsolicited testimony," concluded Baker. "Nobody asked those people if they had a paranormal experience. The experience itself moved them to write those notes."

Hundreds of letters are kept in Baker's database. One note, written on New Year's Day in 2006, talked about an encounter with Jerusha in the wee hours of the night on January 1. "They say you only appear to men, but both my wife and I heard you," wrote one anonymous guest. "After seeing a jagged beam of white light and hearing your strange knocking, we managed to drift back to sleep. You have made us question our beliefs in the supernatural and the structure of life. Your presence has confirmed for us that we are not alone."

NATHANIEL HAWTHORNE

Did local Nathaniel Hawthorne, author of the classics *The Scarlet Letter* and *The House of the Seven Gables*, believe in ghosts? Based on the themes he explored in his books, the iconic author may have, but he definitely had a healthy dose of skepticism.

His friend William Baker Pike worked with Hawthorne at the Salem Custom House in the 1840s. Pike, a Swedenborgian spiritualist, strongly believed in the idea of communicating with the dead. However, the author initially had his doubts. "Hawthorne was a skeptic, but he treated Pike's belief with respect," wrote Margaret Moore in *The Salem World of Nathaniel Hawthorne*.

In fact, Hawthorne wrote about his skepticism in a letter to Pike dated July 24, 1851. "I should be very glad to believe that these rappers are, in any one instance, the spirits of the persons whom they profess themselves to be; but though I have talked with those who have had the freest communication, there has always been something that makes me doubt."

While Hawthorne was initially a skeptic, he started to explore the possibility of the existence of spirits in his fiction. His book, *The House of the Seven Gables*, hinted at the supernatural with one character, Alice Pyncheon, being driven mad by a spell and dying from shame. Her spirit haunted the gabled house. Also, the building's original owner, Matthew Maule, makes a postmortem return to his ancestral dwelling in the novel.

Hawthorne's skeptical tune changed later in his life. In a story written in hindsight and published posthumously, the author claimed he had a close encounter with a haunting while hanging out at the Boston Athenaeum, a members-only research facility considered to be the nation's oldest library, founded in 1807. It was a private gentleman's club, hosting luminaries such as Henry Wadsworth Longfellow, Henry David Thoreau and, of course, Hawthorne, who read books and shared ideas.

Yes, it was a gentleman's club, no, it was not *that* kind of gentleman's club.

According to his published account called *The Ghost of Doctor Harris*, the famed writer in residence was eating breakfast one morning at the library's former Pearl Street location when he noticed a familiar face reading the *Boston Post*. It was Dr. Thaddeus Mason Harris, a well-known Unitarian clergyman from Dorchester, sitting in his usual chair in front of the library's second-floor fireplace. Hawthorne didn't bother the old patriarch. However, he was shocked to learn later that night that the Athenaeum regular had passed away.

Hawthorne returned to the Athenaeum the following day and noticed, completely in shock, Harris sitting at his usual spot and reading the newspaper. Hawthorne had spotted the deceased doctor, looking "gaseous and vapory," and he was completely dumbfounded.

According to lore, Hawthorne spotted Harris's ghost for six weeks, and he later told his editor that he wished he had confronted the apparition. He wanted to ask him what it was like to be dead or at least find out if the old man knew he had passed. In fact, Hawthorne joked with his editor about the Harris encounter, saying, "Perhaps he finally got to his obituary and realized he was dead."

When the library moved to its current posh 10½ Beacon Street location across from the Massachusetts State House in 1847, Harris's ghost reportedly followed the Athenaeum's antiquarian books and his own nineteenth-century portrait. In fact, Harris's misty apparition has been spotted waiting to take the elevator to the structure's top floor.

"Most people believe this to be the ghost of the reverend that Hawthorne saw many years ago," remarked Christopher Forest in *Boston's Haunted History*. "The library was moved from that Pearl Street location to the present-day location near the Boston Common decades ago. However, it would appear that didn't stop the dear Reverend Harris from following the books and moving to the new library. Many people think Harris still rides an elevator to the third floor, so many years after he last visited the old building."

The Boston Athenaeum now opens its red door to the public in guided tours. However, the so-called haunted elevator is off limits to visitors, wrote *Ghosts of Boston Town* author Holly Nadler.

"The public is barred from using the haunted elevator, which rises and falls of its own accord as if prankish spirits amuse themselves by flitting in and out of the cabin, pushing buttons for all five floors," Nadler mused. "According to Boston ghost hunter Jim McCabe, thousands of dollars have been poured into fixing the elevator's unending glitches, to no avail."

In 2002, the Athenaeum bought a brand-new elevator—and it's still acting up. Recent visitors who toured the library contend that the lift still has a mind of its own.

HAWTHORNE'S HAUNT: OLD BURYING POINT

SALEM, MA—History and mystery oozes from the oldest burial ground in Salem. Also known as the Charter Street Cemetery, the Old Burying Point dates back to 1632, contains the remains of 347 bodies, and is the second-oldest cemetery in the country. In addition to its historical relevance, it was a regular haunt for Salem's native son, Nathaniel Hawthorne.

Buried in the Charter Street Cemetery is Hawthorne's ancestor John Hathorne, a witch-trials magistrate whose memory haunted the author. According to local lore, Hawthorne supposedly added the "w" to his name to distance himself from his infamous great-great grandfather. While we know *The Scarlet Letter* writer abhorred his familial connection to the 1692 witch-trials hysteria, there is no evidence that the name-change story is true.

At least eight members of Hawthorne's family were interred there, including his grandparents and two of their daughters. Witch-trials judge Bartholomew Gedney, poet Anne Bradstreet, architect-carver Samuel McIntire, and Mayflower passenger Richard More are also buried there. No surprise, but names from the gravestones in the Charter Street Cemetery often appear in Hawthorne's writings. For example, the small gravestone of Hepzibah Packer, who died in 1885, possibly inspired Hawthorne to use the unusual name of Hepzibah in his novel *The House of the Seven Gables*. The same novel also features a character called "John Swinnerton," who shares his name with a real-life Salem doctor buried in the cemetery in the late seventeenth century. The cemetery was also featured in Hawthorne's *Dr. Grimshawe's Secret.*

The Salem-bred author met his wife, Sophia Peabody Hawthorne, at a lavish dinner party at the Peabody family home at 53 Charter Street, literally next door to the Old Burying Point. Today it's known as the Grimshawe House. According to lore, Sophia suffered from migraines, and the couple would take midnight strolls in the cemetery. It's believed that the headaches were the result of drugs her father, a Salem dentist, prescribed to her during early childhood to ease her difficulty with teething. The Peabody family lived there between 1835 and 1840 before they moved to Boston.

Today the Old Burying Point lies adjacent to the Witch Trials Memorial, a small park dedicated in 1992 to honor the memory of the men and women who were executed for witchcraft in 1692. The Grimshawe House, now in disrepair, stands as an eerie reminder of Salem's nineteenth-century grandeur.

As far as paranormal activity, the Charter Street Cemetery is the usual finale for Salem-based ghost tours. Sensitives claim to have an overwhelming feeling of sadness and depression walking through the graveyard and the adjoining Witch Trial Memorial. Some believe the area is tied to a disaster. According to lore, a former inn on Charter Street caught on fire, and a woman and her son escaped while her husband remained inside to put out the blaze. They ran back in for him, but he was dead.

"In the back corner near Murphy's Restaurant and Bar, a woman in a Victorian-era, powder blue dress can be seen holding a picnic basket, and a young boy in short pants, black shirt, and hat is always seen with her," reported the website Witch City Ghosts. "Often cameras malfunction, but when they do operate properly, the pictures capture bight white streaks of light, paranormal orbs and odd mists."

It's believed that the Victorian-era lady in blue and her son died in the nineteenth-century fire. Apparently, the back corner of the cemetery closest to Murphy's Restaurant, which closed in 2018, is a hot spot for the paranormal. "According to legend, a casket once broke through the wall and fell into the building," added Leslie Rule, writing about the restaurant in *When the Ghosts Scream.* "Employees insist it really happened and point to part of the wall that obviously has been patched. No one knows the identity of the ghosts who wander through the restaurant, but some wonder if they may indeed have escaped from the cemetery next door."

Tim Maguire, co-owner of the Salem Night Tour, said he's heard stories and has seen convincing photos supporting claims that a casket did indeed break through the wall at Roosevelt's Restaurant. "It looked like it was a casket of a small child, possibly a girl," he claimed. "The corner of the cemetery near Murphy's Restaurant is where the Irish Catholics were buried. So, I'm not surprised that it's extremely active."

In addition to orbs and full-bodied apparitions spotted in the cemetery, reports suggest that visitors regularly see a "Lady in White." Oddly, she's rarely captured in photos and film. "The cemetery has been the site of the occasional ghostly appearance of a lady in white," wrote Christopher Forest in *North Shore Spirits*. "The ghost itself does not typically appear in person. Rather, it often manifests itself in the form of orbs. It has even appeared as a slight figure in pictures taken at the site."

The Lady in White has been spotted in buildings and even in the parking lot near the Charter Street Cemetery. According to a report from North Andover's *Eagle-Tribune* in October 2001, the former owner of Roosevelt's Restaurant (the current spot of Murphy's Restaurant and Bar) said he spotted a female apparition when he was working alone in the restaurant at 3:00 a.m. "I was on the second floor," recalled Henry McGowan. "I actually looked up and saw somebody looking down at me. It was a woman." He did a double take, and the phantom vanished.

So, who is the Lady in White? Within the Witch Trials Memorial, one commemorative stone honors witch trial victims Giles Corey and his wife, Martha. However, his second wife, Mary Corey, was also buried in the Old Burying Point. A small, white gravestone with the words "Mary Corry [sic] wife of Giles" marks her skeletal remains. Historians surmise that Giles was very much in love with his second wife. In fact, she's considered to be the love of his life. Oddly, the lady in white has been seen coming from the general vicinity of her grave marker, and many believe it's her spirit that continues to levitate across the cemetery headed toward the Howard Street Cemetery in the area where her beloved husband was pressed to death.

Based on encounters, Corey's spirit simmers with a postmortem resentment after being crushed to death under a pile of stones more than three hundred years ago. However, if anything has the power to undo the curse unleashed by Corey, it's surely his enduring love for his second wife. Perhaps Mary's spirit is searching for her tortured husband…and if the two spirits finally meet, the curse will be undone. Yes, love exists even in the afterlife.

SYLVIA PLATH

There's no doubt that Sylvia Plath, the tortured author of *The Bell Jar* famous for her collection of posthumously published poems called *Ariel*, was haunted by the ghosts from her past. However, did she somehow conjure her inner demons by using a handmade spirit board that she crafted with her husband, Ted Hughes? Yes, it's possible.

Plath was born in Boston, Massachusetts, on October 27, 1932. Her father was an entomologist and professor and the family lived in the Boston area, on Prince Street in Jamaica Plain and on Johnson Street in Winthrop. The poet's mother, Aurelia, had grown up Winthrop and the neighborhood facing Boston Harbor called Point Shirley was mentioned in Plath's work.

She was eight when she published her first poem in the *Boston Herald* and the journal she kept in her teens helped shape the confessional style she was known for in *The Colossus and Other Poems* and her semi-autobiographical novel, *The Bell Jar*. Plath's father, Otto, died on November 5, 1940, which left an indelible scar on the highly intelligent young writer.

In 1950, Plath was accepted into Smith College and during her junior year she was asked to be the guest editor of *Mademoiselle* magazine in New York City. Many of the events that took place that summer, including a botched suicide attempt, became the inspiration for *The Bell Jar*.

She underwent electroconvulsive therapy for severe depression in 1953 after she swallowed her mother's sleeping pills and hid in a crawl space for three days under her house. She spent the next six months in therapy and recovered in McLean Hospital in Belmont, Massachusetts.

Plath first met poet Ted Hughes on February 25, 1956, at a party during her stint at the University of Cambridge. The couple married on June 16, 1956, outside of London. It was during this time that the couple became entranced with astrology and the paranormal, using a homemade Ouija board.

Al Alvarez, the former poetry editor at the *Observer*, believed that this period in her life ultimately led to her demise. "They played spooky games with the Ouija board and read each other's horoscopes," Alvarez wrote in "How Black Magic Killed Sylvia Plath" in the September 14, 1999, edition of *The Guardian*. "By the end, the pseudo black magic which Ted used cannily to get through to the sources of his inspiration had taken her over," Alvarez remembered.

Plath also used pagan rituals for divination. "When her husband left her for another woman, she took his manuscripts, mixed them with a debris of fingernail parings and dandruff from his desk, and burned them in a witch's ritual bonfire," he explained. "As the flames died down, a single fragment of charred paper drifted on to her foot. On it was the name of the woman he had left her for: Assia."

When Plath consulted the makeshift spirit board, she would connect with a spirit guide named "Pan." Her questions generally focused on her career, like which publisher should she work with for her new book, but it became more personal when she reached out to "Pan" to help craft her poetry.

Seven weeks before her suicide on February 11, 1963, Alvarez visited Plath on Christmas Eve, and the poetry editor hardly recognized the tortured writer when she opened the door. "The bright young American housewife with her determined smile and crisp clothes had vanished along with the pancake makeup, the school-mistressy bun and fake cheerfulness," Alvarez wrote in *The Guardian*. "Her face was wax-pale and drained."

Did her spirit board sessions ultimately lead to her tragic death? I reached out to my friends in the paranormal field and asked the question; the responses were mixed.

Danny Perez, who actually designs spirit boards and sells them as art, said the superstitions associated with the divination device are unfounded. "They can be creepy in an interesting way and I love people's stories and experiences, but I think they're harmless," Perez said. "It was originally designed as a parlor game. At the time it was not appropriate for the opposite sex to be alone or touching. Perhaps it's just a well-designed dating game for those times?"

"I don't touch them personally," explained Brian Gerraughty, a paranormal investigator. "They fall into the category of don't mess with it. I know that other forms of contact can 'open doors' as well, but I've just heard too many bad stories of boards with possible attachments that it's not worth it to me."

Dana Boadway Masson, one of my Wiccan high-priestess friends, said that spirit boards should be used with caution. "I've had bad experiences with them in the past, and I was convinced for decades that they were evil and not to be messed with," Masson said. "Now that I've had years of training in communication and protection, I feel that they are no more dangerous than any other form used to communicate. For any kind of divination, all are potentially dangerous if used without proper knowledge and procedure."

PLATH'S HAUNT: DEER ISLAND

BOSTON, MA—Sylvia Plath was haunted by the ghosts of her childhood in Winthrop. In fact, a visit to her father's grave at the Winthrop Cemetery later prompted Plath to write the poem "Electra on Azalea Path." Directly abutting the peninsula's Point Shirley is Deer Island, a stretch of land marred by tragedy and stained with the blood of hundreds of innocents who were confined in one of the most horrific untold genocides in American history.

For the Native Americans quarantined on the 185-acre dumping ground, Deer Island was known as Devil's Island.

A group of native people were converted to Christianity by the Reverend John Eliot. Known as the "praying Indians," they were captured one night in October 1675 and quarantined on the barren island, their captors fueled by fear of the impending King Philip's War. Eliot, a British minister who had fled to Boston in 1631, had painstakingly translated the Bible into their native tribal language. Many of the innocent men, women, and children were holding their Bibles when they were forced to fend for themselves on what was then a desolate island.

"Deer Island became a place of internment in the winter of 1675-76 for approximately 500 Native Americans, whom Europeans had removed from their homes and villages," reported the National Park Service's website. "Many of the imprisoned Native Americans died that winter without access to adequate food or shelter."

Contrary to the NPS report, there were up to 1,100 "praying Indians" kept on Deer Island, and historians believe that more could have lived there who went unrecorded. The Native Americans, demonized by the colonists, were dropping at an alarming rate. Many of them were on the shoreline praying for God to help. No one came.

Reverend Eliot made several attempts to deliver food, but the angry townspeople stopped him by trying to capsize his vessel. A group of men planned to massacre the natives or, as Malden's Abram Hill worded it, to "destroy ye Indians." The rogue slayers never made it out to Deer Island. However, hundreds of natives died anyway from the elements and lack of food.

During the spring of 1676, a rescue vessel was sent to retrieve the few "praying Indians" who were still alive. The handful who did survive were rumored to have been sold as slaves.

Paranormal investigators believe this tragedy left an aura of disaster on Deer Island. People have reported inexplicable cries and a residual haunting of tribal drums on the island over the years. However the screams of the Native Americans were just a precursor to the horrors yet to unfold on this cursed land.

When millions fled Ireland to seek refuge from the Great Famine in the mid-1800s, Deer Island became a quarantine facility for thousands of Irish immigrants. "In June 1847, the City of Boston established a hospital on Deer Island," confirmed the NPS website. "Approximately 4,800 men, women and children were admitted for treatment in the years from 1847 to 1849. Many recovered, but more than 800 died."

There's one notorious haunting in Boston tied to hundreds of Irish children whose lives ended abruptly on Deer Island. According to lore, a teen spirit with a soiled dress has been a regular visitor at the Central Burying Ground. She's believed to be one of the many children buried in a mass grave in the pauper cemetery on the corner of Tremont and Boylston Streets.

According to the late, great ghost expert Jim McCabe, the young spirit is a girl "with long red hair, sunken cheekbones and a mud-splattered gray dress on." On a rainy afternoon in the 1970s, she paid a visit to a dentist named Dr. Matt Rutger, who reportedly experienced "a total deviation from reality as most of us know it." According to Holly Nadler's *Ghosts of Boston Town*, Rutger was checking out the gravestone carvings. He felt a tap on his shoulder and then a violent yank on his collar. No one was there.

As Rutger was bolting from the cemetery, he noticed something out of the corner of his eye. "I saw a young girl standing motionless in the rear corner of the cemetery, staring at me intently," he said. The mischievous spirit then reappeared near the graveyard's gate, almost fifty yards from the initial encounter. Then the unthinkable happened. "He somehow made it by her to Boylston Street, and even though he couldn't see her, he felt her hand slip inside his coat pocket, take out his keys and dangle them in midair before dropping them," McCabe recounted.

Others have spotted the teen spirit over the years. I've seen photos of a full-bodied apparition of what appears to be a girl wearing a bonnet. According to legend, Dr. Rutger was doing an etching at a mass grave for children who died from tuberculosis on Deer Island. For the record, a cemetery on the island called Rest Haven is believed to be the final resting spot for the people who died on the island in the 1800s. However, ghost lore enthusiasts claim the ghost girl regularly encountered in Central Burying Ground is one of the thousands of Irish immigrants who fled to Boston to seek refuge.

In 1850 an almshouse, or asylum for the poor, was built on Deer Island to house the city's paupers. The structure became a short-term prison in 1896. The facility was a house of correction until 1991. According to *A Short History of Nearly Everything*, experiments were done on the prisoners. The facility generally held short-term offenders whose crimes ranged from public drunkenness to disorderly conduct.

According to people who spent time in the Deer Island House of Industry, cruel and unusual punishment was the norm. In fact one woman reached out to *Haunted Boston Harbor* to help solve what is believed to be the unsolved murder of her great, great grandfather. "His name was John Barry. He was murdered in April 1894 on Deer Island where he had been on and off for about 15 years," wrote Julie H. via email. "The *Boston Globe* articles I unearthed helped me confirm he is my ancestor. However, not long after the murder the 'case' went cold and I assume the suspect was never captured. There is nothing about the murder other than the suspects name on the date of the murder and the word 'escaped.'"

Escaped? No reports of a prison escape in 1894 have been found. Besides, based on the structure's design, an escape would be nearly impossible. Based purely on intuition, it sounds like an inside job or cover up of sorts. The waterway, known as the Shirley Gut channel, that separates Deer Island from Winthrop was filled in after the 1938 New England nor'easter. So, it's highly unlikely a prisoner could have escaped the facility and then swum in the harbor without getting caught.

In fact, there was an attempted escape in 1933 and all four men were apprehended.

As far as ghosts are concerned, there's a legend involving the Deer Island Lighthouse, which was built in 1890. "After the Coast Guard took over the light, officer-in-charge John Baxter played a trick on a new crew member," reported LighthouseFriends.com. "Knowing the surf was rising and soon the light would be shaking, he said, 'I want to warn you. We have ghosts out here.' Soon the coffee cup on the table began to dance as if in proof."

Jeremy D'Entremont, historian for the American Lighthouse Foundation, confirmed the ghostly pranks at the Deer Island Lighthouse. "One of the early keepers at Deer Island Light drowned near the lighthouse," he said. "Later, Coast Guard keepers would tell new arrivals that the place was haunted. One told me that he made a coffee cup slide across a table and convinced a new arrival that the ghost did it. Of course, the fact that the whole place was on a slight slant is what made the coffee cup slide."

As D'Entremont mentioned, one tragedy at the Deer Island Lighthouse could have resulted in an actual haunting. Joseph McCabe accepted the post as assistant lightkeeper in 1908. He found the isolation unbearable and had a piano delivered to the lighthouse to "break the monotony of the lonely life in the isolated tower," reported the *Boston Globe* in 1913. He met a woman, Gertrude Walter, in East Boston and left his post on February 16, 1916, to help his soon-to-be-wife address wedding invitations. On the trek back, he hopped on a rock and tragically slipped. McCabe fell into the turbulent Boston Harbor waters and the twenty-eight-year-old lightkeeper's body was never found.

The lighthouse was replaced with a spark plug light in 1982. The Deer Island Sewage Treatment Plant, boasting 150-feet-tall sludge digesters, opened in 1995 and became fully operational in 2000. The facility is responsible for purifying the toxic waters of Boston Harbor.

However, the sounds of the treatment facility can't drown out the postmortem cries of the hundreds who died on the land the Native Americans called Devil's Island.

WILLIAM JAMES

What if an internationally famous professor of psychiatry at Harvard suddenly announced that he believed in ghosts? William James, the wicked smart man responsible for *The Varieties of Religious Experience* in 1890 and Henry's older brother risked it all to scientifically prove that ghosts and psychic phenomenon do exist.

James and his small group of scientist friends could be considered the original *Ghost Hunters*. Unfortunately, he didn't have access to the equipment used by modern investigators. But, that didn't stop him.

Early in his career, James was trained as a physician and even taught anatomy classes at Harvard, but never practiced medicine. Instead, he pursued his interests in psychology and then philosophy. "I originally studied medicine in order to be a physiologist, but I drifted into psychology and philosophy from a sort of fatality. I never had any philosophic instruction, the first lecture on psychology I ever heard being the first I ever gave," James mused in Ralph Barton Perry's *The Thought and Character of William James*.

Riddled with various ailments and often suicidal, James was considered to be the father of American psychology thanks to his groundbreaking approach. He considered associationism, the idea that each experience in life leads to another, as "psychology without a soul." His book, *The Principles of Psychology*, introduced the concept of "stream of consciousness," which later became a literary device used by authors such as James Joyce and William Faulkner.

As far as his work with the paranormal, James was initially hushhush. In fact, he discreetly used an assumed name even though Victorian-era Spiritualism was fashionable at the time. As author Deborah Blum points out in her 2006 book, *Ghost Hunters*, James eventually became passionate about his paranormal pursuits. His mission was to find definitive proof of the existence of life after death.

"Most people believe that he really became engaged [with the paranormal] after the death of his baby son, Herman, who died in 1884," said Blum in an interview in *The Harvard Gazette* in October 2014.

Stricken with grief, James reached out to the American trance medium Leonora Piper. "James came to believe that she knew things about him and his dead child that she couldn't have known without some supernatural ability," said Blum in *The Gazette* interview. "He visited Piper many times to observe and measure her behavior during trances, and while he didn't find that she was always perfect, he did continue to find evidence that convinced him that she somehow knew things, often personal, that she shouldn't have known."

James periodically studied Piper's abilities until his death in August 1910. It was during this period that he became a founding member of the American Society for Psychical Research in Manhattan.

"A lot of his studies involved controlled observations of Piper," Blum told *The Gazette*. "He often sent people to her anonymously and asked them to report on what she told them. One of my favorites of those stories involves a Harvard scientist who gave her a fake name and asked her to tell him what was engraved in a ring that he had received from his mother. She did. He wrote to James in complete bafflement."

Of course, it was culturally acceptable at the time for scientists to study metaphysical phenomenon in the late nineteenth century. "Harvard was very steadfast in supporting him," Blum explained. "You'd never see that today."

JAMES'S HAUNT: KIRKLAND STREET

CAMBRIDGE, MA—You've heard of The Amityville Horror? Well, Cambridge had its own version known as the "Kirkland Street Nightmare." The Treadwell-Sparks House located at 21 Kirkland Street was originally built in 1838 and was moved from Quincy Street to its current location in 1968. However, the house that stood there before had a haunted history that made headlines in the *Boston Daily Globe* on April 8, 1878.

Over a fifteen-year span, tenants at the original house would come and go without giving any explanation. There were reports of disembodied voices, and after a series of revolving-door dwellers, the double-decker was abandoned for years because of its "haunted house" reputation. College students threw rocks through the windows, and stressed-out Harvard kids would squat at the dilapidated house for a spooky night out. In 1878 a man described as Mr. Marsh and his family rented the homestead for fifteen dollars a month and shrugged off the rumors that the house was haunted.

Soon Marsh started hearing his name called out by a demonic, disembodied voice. He also watched in horror as the handle of his door slowly turned and opened when no one, at least among the living, was in the room. After close encounters with an unseen force, the man organized a Victorian-style séance. During the spiritual intervention, Marsh's wife allegedly became possessed by the so-called spirit haunting the house. Mrs. Marsh described in detail the story of an orphan girl who was forcibly taken into the home by a carriage where she was, according to the report, "foully dealt with, murdered and buried in the cellar below the house." During the séance, the spirit said her name was Bertha.

After a few months without paranormal activity, the house's freaked-out tenants started hearing odd noises in the home and up the stairs. They also heard the sounds of glass shattering in the kitchen, yet nothing was broken. The maid claimed she heard "terrible noises" at night and said the furniture in the room was pushed by invisible hands. She also recalled hearing blood-curdling shrieks and cries from a female voice.

After the initial article called "The Spook Roost" appeared in the *Globe*, former residents recalled seeing a full-bodied apparition of a young girl. They recounted objects, like plates on the kitchen table, moving when no one was there. Hundreds of curious spectators gathered around the Kirkland Street house at night while Mr. Marsh dug in the cellar to find the remains of the supposedly murdered girl known as Bertha.

Bones were found in the basement. However, a former tenant claimed that he would bury slaughtered animal bones in the cellar. Investigators couldn't tell if the remains were human or animal. In 1878, police didn't have the forensic and DNA tools investigators use today.

The Marshes, after undergoing public scrutiny because of the reports in the *Globe*, stopped talking to the press and demanded privacy. After several years, they fled the haunted house on Kirkland Street, and it was eventually demolished.

A former maid, Mary Nolan, confirmed the alleged haunting to the *Globe*. "Often I heard the carriage drive up, stop and then go on again. Why, that was quite common. We would hear the sound of wheels, the hoofs of the horses and sometimes the crack of the whip but nothing could be seen. I wouldn't live in that house again for $1,000," Nolan said. "It was enough to frighten people to death."

The late Reverend Peter Gomes, a prominent Harvard theologian and author who lived in the Treadwell-Sparks House until his passing, commented about the ghost lore surrounding Divinity Hall. The Kirkland Street house is near Harvard Divinity. "It was said that if you heard strange noises by the chapel or saw someone there you didn't recognize, it was probably a ghost," Gomes said, adding that the spirits were believed to be "benign, doubtless Unitarian, rational ghosts." Gomes never commented on the female spirit allegedly haunting his home on Kirkland Street.

William James—a Harvard luminary and founder of the American Society for Psychical Research, which is one of the oldest organizations exploring the paranormal—lived at 95 Irving Street, which is a stone's throw from the Kirkland Street haunt. His first essay for the society was about a girl who mysteriously vanished from her home in Enfield, New Hampshire. James investigated the haunting premonitions of Nellie Titus, who allegedly predicted how the sixteen-year-old died on Halloween in the late 1800s. According to the essay, Titus strongly believed that the girl drowned near a Shaker-style bridge in Enfield. Her body was found, but the case continues to be a mystery.

The dead girl's name? Bertha Huse.

GHOST Q&A: GARE ALLEN

"As ghost writers, it's our duty to document these events."
—Gare Allen, *Ghost Crimes*

Gare Allen, a Florida-based author armed with more than a dozen paranormal-themed books, revealed to me that he was pushed to his limits writing about one horrific case featured in *Ghost Crimes*.

"I'm a huge advocate of animal welfare. For me, writing about any kind of animal neglect or abuse is painful," Allen said. "In *Ghost Crimes*, there's a case where an animal is sacrificed in a disturbing fashion, and I had to stop several times to complete writing the scene. Just the thought of an animal being hurt breaks my heart."

When asked about any real-life experience that has terrified him the most, Allen said his encounter with a demonic entity at his new home near Tampa, Florida, inspired him to write *The Dead: A True Paranormal Story*. "I was unprepared for the unholy encounter that would haunt me for the rest of my life," he wrote in *The Dead*. "I opened my eyes to see a grossly burned demon staring coldly at me. Its face was hot red with burned folds of skin running from its forehead down to its neck. Piercing yellow eyes targeted a palpable

PHOTO COURTESY GARE ALLEN.

155

hate at me. The demonic being was only inches from my face and reeked of sulfur."

Waking up to a non-human entity in the wee hours of the night? Yes, that's scary.

"If coming face-to-face with a demon wasn't enough to rank as the most dangerous situation I have ever found myself in, the feeling of complete paralysis and vulnerability helped it to remain my most terrifying experience to date," Allen continued.

The *Ghost Crimes* author weighed in about his lifelong belief in ghosts and what it's really like to write a "based on a true story" novel. While the subject matter that he explores in his books can be fodder for nightmares, it was Allen's real-life close encounter with a malevolent entity that continues to haunt him the most.

Q: Were you ever a skeptic when it comes to the paranormal? If so, what caused you to become a believer?
A: I don't recall ever being a skeptic. Of course I had my first paranormal experience when I was twelve years old, so that didn't allow much time to close off my mind.

One night I went to bed and after only lying down for a few minutes my bed levitated itself. It floated, wobbled, and dropped back down to the floor. I froze in terror.

Two things then happened that told me I wasn't dreaming or imaging the event. The family dog was at the foot of the bed and jumped off in a panic. A few seconds later my older brother came to my door and asked me what the loud sound was.

Q: For people new to the paranormal, what sort of dangers do we face and how do we pick up these entities along the way?
A: Imagine walking into a darkened room with none of your physical senses available to you. You can't see, hear, smell, or physically touch anything, yet you are certain you are not alone. A ghost is with you.

Is it a ghost with benevolent or malevolent intentions? Do they have the ability to manifest and manipulate physical objects? What does the ghost want? With no answers to your questions your heart quickly sinks in the deafening silence and your mind races with thoughts of the worst case scenario.

Everything needs to be fed. Whether it's the bodily replenishment of food and water or the spiritual and emotional need of an energy exchange, our instinctual drive to survive sends us in a continual search of sustenance. For those of us starved for answers to the paranormal world, our energies can light up their alternate sky like the Fourth of July. I can't imagine the energy it must take for a ghost to manifest and move physical objects. But I can attest to the loss of energy when they plug in for some juice.

It's no different in the physical world. We have all met the person who continually wants more and more of your time, energy, and emotion. While most of us are willing to give of ourselves, it comes at a price. We crash at the end of the day, often skipping meditation and allowing our protective aura to be depleted. Much like the hyenas of the physical world, invisible beings surround us, pulling more and more of our energy. And when our energy is down, we open ourselves to illness or emotional distress, and potential spiritual attacks.

The key is maintaining your emotional and spiritual balance to keep your energy field strong. Consistent meditation along with visual exercises are vital to keep yourself protected.

Q: *Ghost Crimes* is based on actual paranormal cases. Was it difficult to walk the line between fiction and non-fiction?
A: It's always tricky to write a story that's based on actual events. As a writer, I always strive to maintain the integrity of the story. With *Ghost Crimes*, I wanted to honor those who actually lived—or in some cases—didn't survive.

Much of the fiction is used to give impact and more depth to the characters or secondary stories that aren't directly impacting the true events. It's nothing short of a dance between fact and fiction but readers, myself included, are more moved by the tale of a true story, especially a paranormal one.

Q: As someone who has been in many dangerous situations, is there one that stands out?
A: The most terrifying situation happened soon after I purchased my home. Within days of unpacking, I discovered that the previous owner had killed himself in the front bedroom. While unsettling, it did explain the items that went missing and never turned up, the movement of objects from one side of the room to another, and even the violent swinging of window blinds with no air flow or explanation.

What I didn't know at the time was that the individual had practiced dark magic and had conjured a demon [that] had remained in my home. I immediately called a psychic friend and he came over to help me cleanse the house with sea salt, holy water, and incense.

Q: Would you recommend investigating to enhance paranormal-themed books?
A: Absolutely. It's clear that the paranormal community wants the same thing and that's answers. What's truly exciting is we all go at it in different ways. Furthermore, we process the information through our filters and that can only, at least eventually, yield a varied and enlightened report of discovery.

Of course, practice protection through meditation, energy work, crystals, sea salt, holy water, and anything that provides vital safety while you search the unknown worlds.

Q: Any words of wisdom for other ghost writers?
A: Remember that we all interpret paranormal life through our own unique perspective. For me, I see things from a left-brained analytical point of view with a heavy emphasis on metaphysics. Paranormal investigators tirelessly gather EVPs and camera footage of physics-defying occurrences. Others rely on messages from beyond through psychic abilities, channeling, and divination.

My hope is that our combined efforts will eventually allow us to finally understand the paranormal world. As ghost writers, it's our duty to document these events.

GHOST ENCOUNTER:
BANISHING THE CRONE

"I'm picking up a woman, a gnarly old witch. Banish her while telling her you're not the one."

—Lucky Belcamino, psychic medium

Leave it to the author of *Wicked Salem* to somehow pick up a cackling crone attachment in Concord, Massachusetts, of all places. For the record, I purposely avoided the Witch City during the month-long *Haunted Happenings* celebration during October 2018 because I needed a ghost break.

No luck. During a spirited stay at Concord's Colonial Inn the weekend before Halloween, I somehow attracted an old hag wanting to latch on to me for a bit. At first I thought I was communicating with a misunderstood female spirit who served as a midwife during the Revolutionary War era. However, she quickly revealed herself to be a shape-shifting trickster.

The crone had plans for me. But I refused to let her hitch a ride. According to my psychic friends who watched this ordeal unfold online during a live investigation, she was attracted to my energy. I somehow picked her up during a midnight stroll in a historic cemetery in Concord.

Confronting a parasitic entity the day before Halloween? Witch, please.

In Concord, I was on the hunt for haunted locations for an upcoming paranormal convention spotlighting the famous authors who lived and died in this peaceful transcendentalist enclave in Massachusetts. When I checked into Concord's Colonial Inn, I was immediately overwhelmed with the lingering energy of the ghosts of the city's tumultuous past.

The spirits of Concord called me. And it was more than the psychic imprint left by the "shot heard 'round the world." The residual energy haunting the inn spans more than three centuries. Based on my initial baseline sweep of the property, several of the ghosts sticking around simply didn't know that they were dead.

"Imagine waking up in the middle of the night to find a Revolutionary War soldier standing at the foot of your bed," author Joni Mayhan warned me before my visit to Concord's Colonial Inn. "Built in 1716, the inn is located just down the road from the North Bridge, where the Battles of Lexington and Concord occurred. During the Revolutionary War, a portion of the inn was used to store firearms and provisions for the militia. Another section was the office of Dr. Thomas Milot. Wounded soldiers were brought to his office during the battle, and many succumbed to their injuries, lending truth to the ghostly encounters."

Converted to an inn around 1889 and renamed Concord's Colonial Inn eleven years later, the hotel was home to Henry David Thoreau, famous for his "Civil Disobedience" essay and, of course, *Walden*. Thoreau lived in the inn while he attended Harvard. The eighteenth-century structure served as a boarding house before being transformed into a hotel called the Thoreau House, named after the famous writer's aunts.

"When I had the opportunity to investigate the inn years ago, I wasn't disappointed by the activity," Mayhan told me. "While we didn't see the soldier materialize in the bedroom, we did witness strange tapping sounds, shadows moving, and odd smells appearing out of nowhere. While conducting an EVP session in an attempt to get the resident ghosts to speak to us through our digital recorders, a lacy doily flew off the back of a chair and landed on my head, surprising me."

After checking into my supposedly non-haunted room, I had a long conversation with the Colonial Inn's night auditor, Aaron. His own personal experience with the notoriously haunted inn's ghosts involved a radio turning on by itself. No surprise but there were no batteries in the electronic device.

As the conversation progressed, the front-desk employee told me that a guest checked into the haunted room 24 during his shift. According to his story, the woman fled her room after hearing someone say, "Boo!" ten minutes after she said the lights in the room mysteriously turned off, and a disembodied voice said, "Get out." Of course, the freaked-out guest did.

The night auditor mentioned that employees often hear voices in the inn's main dining area called Merchants Row. "The older employees always seem to experience the inn's ghosts," he told me. "Not the younger workers."

Aaron told me he feels uncomfortable walking into Merchants Row at night. "I can't explain it, but it feels like I'm walking into a den of bears." Apparently Aaron doesn't want to poke the bear.

The Concord Colonial Inn (circa between 1910 and 1920).
PHOTO FROM THE LIBRARY OF CONGRESS.

I asked if employees have spotted an elderly female spirit in the hotel and he confirmed my hunch. Aaron said she has been spotted lounging in a chair in the sitting room on the main floor next to the creepy paintings. When I walked by, I got the chills because I could see her in my mind's eye.

After my chat with Aaron, I decided to check out Concord at night and walked to the nearby Old Hill Burying Ground in Monument Square. Originally next to Concord's first meetinghouse, the graveyard is more than three hundred years old. According to superstition, it was bad luck to transport a corpse over flowing water, so the community created South Burying Ground on the opposite side of Mill Brook. For years, the Monument Square cemetery was known as North Burying Ground.

As soon as I walked up to the historic cemetery, I felt as if I was being watched. In fact, I somehow picked up something sinister from what locals call the "skull tombstone" at Old Hill Burying Ground. "According to the lore, there's an eerie aura throughout the 1700s burying ground," reported *Concord Patch*'s Patrick Ball. "The spookiest site is an old tombstone with a strange skull image and equally unsettling 'bowing to the king of terror' inscription. Some report seeing 'real' eyes inside the skull's sockets, which appear to follow visitors as they move around."

After my midnight stroll, I headed back to Concord's Colonial Inn to report on my "creepy as hell" experiences out in the cemetery. As soon as I walked into my room and turned on my computer, I intuitively knew I wasn't alone. Holding my trusty dowsing rods charged for spirit communication, I set up an online video chat with my Facebook friends. I was hoping that my fellow empaths from the psychic community could figure out who, or what, was in the hotel room with me.

Oddly, my computer kept turning on and off. Issues with electronic devices, based on first-hand experience, is usually a sign that something wicked this way comes.

"There's a woman in the room," said Luis Escalera, a gifted spirit medium with the ability to remotely see the ghosts that I connect with at some of New England's most haunted locations. "She's in the corner not wanting to be seen or heard. She's just curious."

The psychics watching the live feed believed the spirit was possibly a nurse from the eighteenth century. However, my computer screen kept freezing and my friends were picking up all sorts of conflicting activity. "What happened to the video feed? I was going to say that the spirit is related to something medical," commented empath Cynthia Mattison. "She was a midwife in her forties. It was often confused [with witchcraft] because of the herbs and women were supposed to suffer pain for childbirth."

Several people watching the live video, including Escalera, told me that the entity kept changing form and was possibly a shapeshifter. The spirit medium warned, "Do you know that you're talking to a trickster?"

Escalera was right. When I asked the entity to present itself to me, I realized that I was connecting with a crone, an elderly woman often portrayed in pop culture as a wise witch with magical powers. Apparently, the entity had a sense of humor. "Could you be more stereotypical?" I joked with the shapeshifting entity. She cackled.

Several of my psychic friends who watched the series of online videos recommended that I leave the inn immediately. "She's intrigued by your energy," said psychic Kristen Cappucci. "She will try to mess with you tonight."

After communicating with the witch ghost, I headed downstairs for some fresh air because I couldn't sleep. As I walked into the lobby area, I clearly heard a male voice whisper in my ear, "Right behind you."

I jumped and said, "Oh, you scared me." But when I turned around, there was nobody there. The night auditor was on the second floor. I was completely creeped out, but I was exhausted. I decided to crash in my room for the night despite multiple warnings from my psychic-medium friends.

As I tossed and turned in my bed, the crone wouldn't leave me alone. She kept sitting on my chest. Known as a "night hag," the malevolent entity from folklore has been associated with sleep paralysis or night terrors. It's a phenomenon of feeling immobilized by an unseen force.

The traumatic night was on replay and repeated itself several times throughout my sleep. I would wake up, unable to move and feeling as if I was pinned to the bed. Finally, after an intense struggle and raising myself from the bed, I would gasp for air. After about three visits from the night hag, I begged her to leave me alone. She eventually listened and I managed to get about an hour of sleep.

After checking out of Concord's Colonial Inn, I found myself in such a cross mood. Something was wrong. I felt as if I was just a vessel and the ghost-witch entity was sort of running the show. It was very similar to an attachment I picked up in the past, but this one was less dangerous.

The first clue to the fact that I was not alone was the food I ordered for breakfast. Eggs Benedict? I'm not a hollandaise sort of guy. The second was ordering tea. I'm sorry, but that is so not me. I'm strictly coffee in the morning. Finally, the entity was determined to express to management that she was unhappy with a few things at the hotel when I checked out. She didn't like some of the furniture at Concord's Colonial Inn.

The crone was trying to hitch a ride with me back to Boston. I reached out to my friends in the paranormal community for help. My psychic-medium friend, Lucky Belcamino, identified the entity immediately.

"I'm picking up a woman, a gnarly old witch," she told me. "Banish her while telling her you're not the one. She thinks you did something to her."

Belcamino is gifted when it comes to dealing with negative entities. In fact, her experience as the official psychic of the Lizzie Borden B&B in Fall River has exposed her to some of the darker spirits lurking in the shadows of New England's most haunted locations.

When I asked her how to banish the crone, she said, "Put some white salt around your feet in a circle. Leave her at the gallows in Salem if you get a chance to go. Put her on an imaginary ship." This would be done by conjuring an image of a ship in my mind's eye and somehow convincing the entity to board.

It was the night before Halloween and I didn't have time to travel to Salem and banish the crone. My issue was that I was hosting a ghost-story event at the Somerville Theatre, close to my home in Assembly Square. What was a bit unnerving about the entity is that I could hear her cackling. She even whispered my name in my ear. She was a talkative ghost witch.

At the Somerville Theatre, the crone kept quiet for the most part. Several of my psychic friends who watched the online videos at Concord's Colonial Inn were at the event and sensed that she was still with me. In fact, Cappucci told me she was standing behind my left shoulder.

I decided to talk about my issues with the attachment to the group. At the end of the evening when the attendees left the room, I heard her voice loud and clear. "Don't leave me, Sam," she begged.

Even though I was completely exhausted, I didn't sleep much that night. In the morning, Halloween day, I decided to do the unthinkable—I made plans to go to Salem, Massachusetts, on the busiest night of the year.

The Witch City on All Hallow's Eve? Now, that's scary.

My friend Andy agreed to make the trek with me to banish the crone at the gallows. Salem was packed with costumed revelers and we had to navigate through thousands of dressed-up partygoers. However, we were on a mission.

At a witch shop in Pickering Wharf, I purchased some last-minute supplies, including sea salt, Florida Water for the cleansing and protection ritual, Paolo Santo for smudging, and two obsidian or jet rocks to absorb the negative energy. Earlier that evening, I had reached out to my high-priestess friend to help me plan out the ritual, which would be carried out behind the Walgreens in the Gallows Hill neighborhood.

Armed with a bag of smudging tools, we headed to the execution site.

In 2016 a group of scholars confirmed Proctor's Ledge as the location where nineteen innocent people accused of witchcraft were hanged more than three centuries ago. Two years after making the public announcement, the city dedicated a memorial for the victims near the wooded, city-owned area that abuts Proctor and Pope Streets. Officials unveiled the memorial on July 19, 2017, commemorating the anniversary of the execution of Rebecca Nurse, Sarah Good, Elizabeth Howe, Susannah Martin and Sarah Wildes.

The crescent-shaped granite memorial was eerily quiet around midnight on Halloween. For the record, the site is off-limits after dark, so we were technically not supposed to be there. First my friend and I held hands and said a protection prayer. I could hear the crone's voice whispering in the wind. Then I created a magic circle out of sea salt and demanded that the ghost witch detach from my energy field.

The Concord Colonial Inn circa between 1910 and 1920.
PHOTO FROM THE LIBRARY OF CONGRESS.

"I'm not the one," I said out loud. I invoked Archangel Michael and asked my ancestors to banish but not bind her. "You are now free," I said. I visualized an imaginary vessel and then demanded that she take the ship to be with her people. The wind mysteriously started to gust and the trees overlooking Gallows Hill seemed to dance in the moonlight.

The last thing I heard was "leave" from the voice from beyond, as if she accepted that I had to cut the cord but she was a little sad that I had to set her free. I said my goodbyes and Andy left the jet rock at the Proctor's Ledge memorial.

The banishing ritual worked. I haven't heard from my ghost-witch attachment since sending her off on an imaginary cruise departing from Salem on Halloween. No more late-night whispers. Not even a cackle.

GHOST PROFILE: PETER BEBERGAL

"The religious occult and the supernatural imagination are essential to what it is to be human."

—Peter Bebergal, *Strange Frequencies*

Don't judge a book by its paranormal-themed cover. Peter Bebergal's *Strange Frequencies* isn't a "how to" guide to using technology to connect with the spirit realm.

Who ya gonna call? Not Bebergal. Ghost hunting isn't his thing.

In *Strange Frequencies*, he's not interested in conjuring the dead or confronting a demon even though he did give both an old-school try. "Computers and the Internet have made a kind of magic that works with a simple mouse click," Bebergal wrote in *Strange Frequencies.* "Literally, hundreds of websites, programs, and smartphone applications function as digital divination devices."

Strange Frequencies is about taking a spiritual journey via technology.

"The genesis of *Strange Frequencies* came out of writing *Season of the Witch*," Bebergal told me in a sit-down interview in Cambridge, Massachusetts. "With that book, I was able to explore the idea of the occult imagination. I wasn't interested in the idea

PHOTO COURTESY PETER BEBERGAL.

that if you play an album backwards that it would somehow summon Satan. I was more interested in why people were doing it in the first place and how they responded to it."

The occult imagination is vast, he explained. It not only includes our desire for divine knowledge, but encompasses the fear of that knowledge.

"People respond to playing the record backwards in different ways," Bebergal continued. "Some might be afraid of it while others may be inspired by it. Some might use it for marketing purposes. Some people may see it as a symbol of rebellion."

In *Season of the Witch*, he argued that magic is, in essence, a spiritual hack. Using this concept, he believed this liminal space he called the occult imagination could also be accessed using technology.

"After looking at the occult imagination in music and pop culture, I wanted to see where else I could trace it," he explained. "Technology was a place where people were using and engaging with it in the same ways. They were using technology to elevate their beliefs and debunk other people's beliefs. But their ultimate purpose was to achieve an altered state of consciousness."

In *Strange Frequencies,* Bebergal experimented with building a spirit radio and an automaton, recording EVPs as well as examining the legend of the Golem from Jewish mysticism. He also explored spirit photography and the relationship with stage magic and the supernatural.

"When I talk about the occult and the supernatural, I purposely avoid anything to do with psychic phenomenon, ESP (extrasensory perception), or human-potential phenomenon. The discussion of those things tends to be binary. It either is or isn't and that's the least interesting conversation to me," he said. "With *Strange Frequencies*, I wanted to write honestly about experiences that I may or may not have had and engage with the people who are using technologies for that very purpose."

In other words, Bebergal isn't debunking some of the more extraordinary cases like William H. Mumler's controversial spirit photographs from the 1860s. "Enchantment is a key word for me because it has to do with a state of being instead of belief. One can be enchanted by something and not believe in the religious notions that made it possible," he explained. "I can be enchanted with one of Mumler's ghost photographs and really engage with it but rationally know that it's a fake."

The fifty-two-year-old author, who grew up in Massachusetts, said he has been interested in the supernatural for years. "I was a child of the seventies and early eighties. I was consumed with anything having to do with magic, supernatural, the occult, and monsters," he said. "Every weekend I would watch *Creature Double Feature* and I read all of the Marvel monster comics."

Did Bebergal ever have a paranormal experience along the way? "Yes, but not in a way that was transformative," he told me. "It was only in ways that made me accept that consciousness and reality aren't always perfectly stable. It could glitch out sometimes."

Apparently, ghosts and other paranormal entities don't act on command. "One of the issues with the occult and the supernatural is that it lends itself to a spiritual schizophrenia," he said. "Why would it work on a Tuesday and not on a Wednesday? I had more profound spiritual experiences that I don't consider paranormal than actual paranormal experiences."

In *Strange Frequencies*, Bebergal wrote about his attempt to communicate with his late father. "I used computers to divine, built an automaton listened over and over to tiny pieces of recordings trying to tease out a message from the dead or some other supernatural entity," he wrote. "I even invited the spirit of my father—whose voice in my head underpinned my skeptical thoughts—to communicate with me through his old reel-to-reel recorder."

When I asked him about the emotional retelling in his book about hearing his father's voice on a previously recorded cassette tape, something weird happened. My recorder mysteriously paused when Bebergal talked about his deceased parents.

"It's happening again," he said when I noticed that my recorder had mysteriously stopped. "Maybe my father doesn't want to go on the record?"

Bebergal said his parents were on two extremes of the spectrum in regards to the paranormal. "My mother was emotional and my father was extremely rational," he explained. "I want to be somewhere in the middle and find a balance. I would call myself a believing skeptic, but there are parts of me that are superstitious, which sometimes rears its head. With my rational side, I have to be careful not to dismiss things that are irrational."

Bebergal grew up outside of Salem and said he remembers waiting for the bus to the Witch City in front of the Swampscott cemetery. "Having that kind of access enabled me to explore my fascination with the occult at an early age," he said.

The author fondly remembers strolling down Essex Street in the Witch City and checking out books about the supernatural that he found in Laurie Cabot's witch shop. "I was trying to weed through the commercialism perpetuated by Salem," he said.

I told Bebergal about my recent chat with Cabot in 2018 discussing the city's coven of commercialism. Cabot, in the interview for my book *Wicked Salem*, talked about poltergeist phenomenon saying that it's a "quirk of energy from the living." In other words, people can manifest "thought forms" without even knowing they are doing it. "A poltergeist is not from another realm," she said. "It's not a ghost or spirit. It's something else."

Bebergal said he's heard of a similar point of view from the folks at the Rhine Research Center. "They believe a poltergeist is a stress-induced event associated with telekinesis," he explained. "The team at the Rhine Research Center also believes that the ghost-hunting culture is detrimental to the real science of investigating and measuring paranormal phenomenon."

Speaking of poltergeists, Bebergal said Steven Spielberg's classic film from 1982 continues to resonate with him. "I still really love the movie *Poltergeist*," he told me. "It's perfect. How did the spirits enter the house? Through technology and it becomes this window to spiritual suburban life."

As far as his passion as an author, Bebergal's goal is to continue exploring this concept of the occult imagination. "I want to say something bigger about enchantment and states of enchantment," he explained. "The religious occult and the supernatural imagination are essential to what it is to be human."

GHOST Q&A: JONI MAYHAN

"My advice to other ghost writers is to be fully aware of what you're getting yourself into. You need to understand the dangers and have a damn good back-up plan."

—Joni Mayhan, Ghost Magnet

Joni Mayhan is an Indiana-based author and paranormal investigator formerly from Massachusetts. She traveled to hell and back while working on her book documenting the extreme hauntings that terrorized the Simpson family living in Hanover, Pennsylvania. "The ghosts there [didn't] want their story told," she said about her site-specific book called *The Hanover Haunting*. "They want[ed] to continue tormenting this family, and view[ed] me as a threat. I indeed put myself into the line of fire for the sake of this story, but I wouldn't have it any other way. It was a story that needed to be told."

Armed with years of experience and several best-selling books, including *Ghost Magnet* and *Signs of Spirits*, Mayhan has a history confronting entities and then writing about them. "After I lived through a severe attachment and documented my experience in my book, *The Soul Collector*, many people contacted me, surprised I continued to investigate the paranormal. They encouraged me to

PHOTO COURTESY JONI MAYHAN.

pull away from anything scary and attempt to recuse myself. Unfortunately, that doesn't work."

In the interview, Mayhan talks about her abilities to connect with the spirits that she writes about and offers advice to up-and-coming authors in the paranormal field. Yes, something wicked this way comes.

Q: You and I both seem to pick up attachments more than your average empath. Any idea why?
A: I believe that some people are beacons. Due to our abilities and the brightness of our auras, we shine a little brighter than most people. This makes us more visible to the other side. Some of them are drawn to us for help, some just want to be with us, and others want to steal our energy. Darker ones recognize our potential to help the other side and want to stop us.

This is why we need to become very practiced with our paranormal protection methods. It's taken me nearly a decade to find something that works for me and it's still not failsafe. While I don't pick up as many attachments as I used to, I still get them from time to time.

Q: What exactly is an attachment?
A: An attachment is a ghost that latches on to a living person. It attaches itself to them and follows them everywhere they go. The stronger ones can alter people's personalities and drain their energy. If given enough time, they can almost completely take a person over.

This is different from a demonic possession, but the two share many traits. Someone with a ghost attachment will begin to suffer personality changes, much like a demonic possession, but they never fully lose themselves. They might feel like they've lost the reins to their life, but they are still there, watching in horror as it transpires. Attachments are far easier to remove than demonic possessions, but they're still tremendously difficult. It usually requires the services of a strong psychic medium or a shaman.

An attachment is different from a typical haunting, too. In a haunting, the ghost takes up residency in the house and affects the people living there. An attachment is only interested in the person it's connected to. They don't usually bang on the walls and move items around to toy with us, they get into our heads instead. It might start out with a stray thought that doesn't feel like your own. If given enough time, the whisper will become a shout, escalating until it becomes your new reality.

Q: You were in a pretty dangerous situation in Pennsylvania. Can you talk about that?

A: I was commissioned to write a book about the *Hanover Haunting*. This is a small, normal-looking brick house in Hanover, Pennsylvania, that is insanely haunted. It's been on many paranormal television shows, including *The Dead Files*.

When DeAnna Simpson contacted me, I knew I was embarking on an incredibly dangerous venture. This house is more than just a house. It's become an entity of its own. The owners frequently see creepy full-body apparitions and have been physically assaulted inside their own home. They would have left the house years ago if they were financially able to. The house keeps them trapped, continually inflicting horrors on a daily basis.

In September of 2018, I visited the house on my way home from a trip to Massachusetts to attend the Plymouth Paracon. I wasn't planning on starting the book until early 2019, but I thought it would be good to see the house beforehand.

I have to admit, I was feeling fairly cocky. Michael Robishaw sent his guides to protect me and my paranormal protection was in place. I played happy music on the way there, trying to keep my vibration as high as possible, and felt bulletproof.

All that ended the minute I walked through the door. My iron-clad bubble of shielding turned into a dishwater soap-bubble and Michael's guides were forced into action. The ghosts were immediately all over me.

I've never been in such a severely haunted house. It was like trying to walk through sludge. The energy was so strong and so hostile; nothing I did worked. My body vibrated like I was attached to a jackhammer as they pulled energy from me. I was supposed to spend the night, but quickly changed my mind.

I contacted Michael and he confirmed my fears. After chatting with the home owners for several hours, I retreated to a local hotel for the night and counted my blessings.

Q: As someone who has been in many dangerous situations, is there one that stands out, and why?

A: When I'm asked about my most dangerous paranormal experience, I always mentally return to *The Soul Collector*. It's not a neat little story about good overcoming evil. It's a tale of caution and lessons learned.

I was born with metaphysical abilities but didn't truly tap into them until I was in my mid-forties. Once I did, I was astounded at what I discovered. It was like being gifted with a fascinating toy. I didn't realize that this new-found plaything came with side effects though.

The more I worked with it, the stronger it got. It was like a muscle that was being exercised. I soon joined a paranormal group and began investigating in earnest. Since I knew where the ghosts were, I was able to collect some fairly astounding EVPs. I was absolutely elated until I ran into a very hostile entity.

He latched onto me with an iron grip and wouldn't let go. My life became a living hell as he attempted to take me over. Friends tried to help me, but he was stronger than all of us put together. It made me realize the importance of paranormal protection and always having a back-up plan for the worst-case-scenario.

As horrible and potentially deadly as the experience was, I'm thankful it happened. It opened the door for my paranormal writing career and started me down the path I'm still following. I've learned so much since then and will continue to grow and learn.

Q: Any words of wisdom for other ghost writers?
A: My advice to other ghost writers is to be fully aware of what you're getting yourself into. You need to understand the dangers and have a damn good back-up plan. If you have children, remember that what comes home with you will also affect them.

We all want to be seen as fearless investigators, but fear is an essential tool too. We should never latch onto fear and allow it to permeate our bodies, but we should always listen to it. We need to respect the fact that there are invisible warriors out there who are intent on bringing us harm. Just because we can't see them doesn't mean they aren't there.

Start slowly and master paranormal protection before you get started. I still can't remove strong attachments by myself. I use talented psychic mediums and one very amazing shaman to help me. Find someone and make sure they have your back. It just might save your life one day.

CONCLUSION

"Do the legwork, visit the locations, research them, format your own conclusions, and share them with the world."
—RICHARD ESTEP, AUTHOR AND PARANORMAL INVESTIGATOR

The most important thing I've learned on my journey writing historical-based ghost books? That I get by with a little help from my friends. The second lesson I learned along the way is that if you play with fire, you'll eventually get burned. The third? Don't die.

Two out of three ain't bad.

On October 30, 2016, I got burned really bad. It happened so fast that it felt like spontaneous combustion. I somehow picked up an attachment after accidentally channeling a spirit at Peirce Farm at Witch Hill in Topsfield, Massachusetts. The entity, later identified as a murderer, eventually possessed me. The terrifying incident is chronicled on the one-hundredth episode of *A Haunting* featured on the Travel Channel.

It's a cautionary tale and a perfect example of what not to do when investigating a haunted location.

If it wasn't for Joni Mayhan, I probably wouldn't have survived the incident. I'm lucky to be alive.

When I filmed the episode of *A Haunting* with Mayhan, I thanked her for intervening during the infestation and alerting Michael Robishaw, the shaman who helped bind and banish the entity. After the Travel Channel show interview, I started to have flashbacks replaying the horrifying, week-long ordeal that almost destroyed me. Mayhan identified with the residual trauma because she went through something similar, which inspired her to write her first book, *The Soul Collector*.

"It was a terrifying experience that a lot of people wouldn't have mentally survived," Mayhan said, trying to comfort me. "It's even harder to get past it because it's paranormal and not an acceptable tragic experience.

People don't understand how scary and life altering it is. Since the *Soul Collector,* I still sleep with a night light. I get really freaked out about sleeping in the dark. I need to know what's around me."

I confessed to Mayhan that I was afraid the entity would come back if I talked about it on television.

"It just brought it all back," she continued. "We push those things into boxes in our heads so we don't have to keep looking at them. Getting them back out of the boxes is hard because they don't lose any of their power. If nothing else, they get stronger."

This initial conversation with Mayhan inspired me to reach out to other paranormal-themed writers about the dangers that we face out in the field. I was surprised to learn that most of the contemporary authors featured in *Ghost Writers* got their start as investigators before penning their first book.

In fact, Richard Estep had many years of experience before writing his first memoir, *In Search of the Paranormal,* in 2015. The author, originally from the United Kingdom, managed to write fifteen successful books in less than four years.

"Almost all of my dangerous experiences as a paranormal investigator have come from the living, not the dead," Estep told me. "There was the time when a local resident of a mountain town approached me when I was investigating a historic theater and asked me if I was cooking meth. When I said that I wasn't, he flashed a handgun and said, 'Good, because we know how to make people disappear around here'," he recalled.

Is it important to Estep to investigate the haunted locations before he writes about them in his books like *The Fairfield Haunting and Trail of Terror*? "I love the storytelling process and that begins with the research and the 'boots on the ground' component of paranormal investigation," he explained. "It's one thing to tell ghost stories that you've gotten from interviewing witnesses; it's another thing entirely to spend a week living, sleeping, and investigating in the place that you're writing about. I think it adds credibility."

Unlike most of the authors featured in this book, Estep tends to gravitate toward single locations—like Malvern Manor in Iowa or Asylum 49 in Utah—boasting enough ghostly material to sustain an entire book. "As my writing career progresses, I enjoy devoting an entire book to a single location," he said. "It feels as though the story has more room to breathe over the space of fifty thousand words than it does when it's compressed into a single chapter. I become very fond of some of the locations I investigate, and like to delve into the lives of those who lived and worked there."

For his single-location books, Estep usually writes the first section at the haunted location he's featuring. "I feel that it helps capture the atmosphere of the place in some small way," he explained. "Each book, or chapter of a book, is a reminder of that time of my life, and takes me right back there when I open up the book months or years later. I hope to one day be an old man who can go to the bookshelf in order to relive some of the high points of my life."

Estep's advice to future ghost writers? "Investigate first and then write about your findings," he said. "Do the legwork, visit the locations, research them, format your own conclusions and share them with the world. The paranormal, non-fiction field needs more good books."

I also reached out to Gare Allen, author of *Ghost Crimes* and *The Dead: True Paranormal Story*, to ask him about his journey. "During my early twenties, I studied metaphysics. I couldn't read enough about astral projection, divination, spirit guides, channeling, and mostly, reincarnation," he told me. "My experiences inspired me to write a series of short stories called *7 Lessons*. All seven books are based on my actual metaphysical and paranormal encounters with fictional insertions to bridge the stories."

Allen's first series of books eventually inspired him to write *The Dead*. "I was often asked if the main character, Greer, was based on me and if the otherworldly events really happened to me," he said. "After fielding that question dozens of times, I decided to chronicle every metaphysical and paranormal event that had occurred in my life including the purchase of a haunted house."

In *The Dead*, Allen comes face-to-face with a demonic infestation in his home. In addition to the lower-level demon, he's also had to combat spirit attachments. Mayhan, who is good friends with Allen, said parasitic entities are one of the many dangers we face as ghost writers.

"I've had attachments latch on to me, but not reveal themselves until a later time," Mayhan explained. "I believe they hide because they have a mission they want to complete and don't want us to be aware of them. If we know they are there, we'll try to disentangle ourselves from them, and they don't want that to happen."

"When [attachments] occur, it's usually a high-level entity, one that has been around long enough to learn the ins and outs. They are also much harder to remove," she said. "Our shaman friend, Michael Robishaw, calls them 'ancient ones' because they have been around for a century or more and have grown powerful over time."

Much like the experience I had with the crone attachment that I banished in Salem, Massachusetts, Mayhan picked up a parasitic entity while doing paranormal research for a book. "I once went to an investigation at a friend's rental house. He knew the house was haunted and often invited close friends over to investigate," she recalled. "The house was located on land that had significance to the Native Americans who lived there centuries ago. While we were outdoors walking around, I picked up an attachment."

Mayhan said that she didn't realize it was an attachment until later that night. "As I was drifting off to sleep, I suddenly felt something pop into the room. My chest grew tight as though something was sitting on me," she said. "I reached out to Michael and he sent his spirit guides to help me. When they arrived, they saw the entity sitting on my chest and trying to push the life out of me. Thankfully, they were able to remove it, but it wasn't a pleasant experience."

As ghost writers, why do we continue to put ourselves in the middle of some disturbingly dangerous situations? Like Mayhan and the other contemporary authors featured in this book, I'm investigating extremely haunted locations and then sharing my experiences—the good and the bad—so that my readers will not make the same mistakes.

What I do know is that there is life after death. I believe it with all of my heart. My pursuits are not to prove that ghosts exist. I'm already convinced. My primary goal is to give a voice to the spirits I encounter along the way, especially those marginalized by the status quo. I want to honor the downtrodden people forgotten by history. I want to give a voice to those without a voice. I want to help people, both the living and the dead.

And if I run into a few hurdles along the way, like getting possessed or levitating out of my bed, so be it. What doesn't kill me, makes me stronger and, ultimately, it makes me a better ghost writer. Period.

DEDICATION

My stepfather, Paul Dutcher, passed the day after Christmas in 2018. He lived and died in beauty. My family held a peaceful "celebration of life" ceremony for him on Navarre Beach in Florida. His death happened while I was writing this book and I want my readers to know how much of an impact this amazing man had on my life.

My sister Angie and I were very young when my mother fled from Chicago and divorced my biological father. We had a tough early childhood after moving back to my mother's hometown in Florida. Paul had just graduated from the University of Michigan in Ann Arbor with a history degree. He was a smart man and was part of the state's anti-war protests.

After graduation, he traveled all over the country, including New England during the fall, and settled in Florida after having a spiritual moment out in the ocean. He told me, when he saw how the moon reflected on the ocean at night, he knew he was home.

He met my mother when they both were employees at one of Pensacola's most haunted locations, Seville Quarter. He was a bartender and she was a waitress. According to my father, it was a love at first sight.

I remember moving in with him at his apartment. I loved that he had a pool and I remember his book collection. The first novel I remember seeing him read was *Shogun*. He loved music, specifically jazz and many of the folk singers from the 1960s. He had an affinity for female vocalists like Joni Mitchell and Joan Baez.

For me, he will always be associated with Christmas because that first one we had together in the 1970s was the best one ever. We went to the movie theater to watch the first *Star Wars* movie. He married my mother on October 14, 1979. Their wedding song was "Clair de Lune." His loved ones from Michigan accepted my sister and me with opened arms. He came from a family of extremely intelligent, progressive, and loving people.

Paul loved playing the piano and taught me and my sister how to play when we were young. As I got older, he supported my creativity. In fact, he typed and edited my first submission to a magazine. I got a rejection from *Highlights* in the third grade. But I will never forget his help with that story.

My mother had three more children and times were tough for us. He bought an old haunted bar called the "Porthole" that ended up catching on fire. We lost everything. However, our livelihood eventually got better and my younger brothers and sisters didn't see the struggles we had when they were very little.

Paul was a substitute teacher at one point and I believe my love for history came from him. He also had a voice that was made for radio and did a lot of voice-over work for a local radio station later on. His baritone voice was one of the best in the business. He was a bartender during my teens and I remember him telling me that he enjoyed being a "barstool psychologist" when he tended bar. He drove a blue hippie van and was always trying to keep the "love van" running.

There was one moment when I was younger that he and I had a heart to heart. I asked him why he married my mother. He paused and, for the first time ever, I noticed a tear roll down his cheek. He said, "Your mother is the most honest woman I have ever known."

We had a house of sensitive souls. He was quiet and laid-back and would always play his jazz music in the background. However, when he spoke, it meant something. His words were powerful. When I asked him where he would go if he could visit any place again based on his days as a hippie who roamed America in his Volkswagen Squareback, he told me he loved Vermont in the fall. I'm dedicating *Ghost Writers* to the man who was my father most of my life and introduced me to the works of many of the authors featured in this book.

ACKNOWLEDGMENTS

When I was younger, my mother would drop me off at the local library so I could do some last-minute research for my history fair projects. I loved spending hours searching through the special collections and the old-school card catalogue at the university's reference center.

It was during that time period that I became a voracious reader. I consumed at least three books a week and fell in love with the words of many of the authors featured in *Ghost Writers*. My first obsession was Edgar Allan Poe. I remember memorizing "The Raven" and then reading most of his famous works like "The Tell-Tale Heart" and "The Cask of the Amontillado." In addition to loving Poe, I was a Stephen King fanatic and I strongly believe that *The Shining* led me into the paranormal field. King's words continue to haunt me.

If you asked me about my favorite books back then, I probably would've rattled off the classics like Nathaniel Hawthorne's *The Scarlet Letter*, Mark Twain's *Huckleberry Finn*, and Charles Dickens's *A Tale of Two Cities*. As my tastes matured, I became enamored with many of the female authors featured in this book, including Sylvia Plath, Shirley Jackson, and Edith Wharton. I read Wharton's *The Age of Innocence* over and over. I was genuinely smitten with the Countess Ellen Olenska and wanted to walk the streets that she and Newland Archer visited. After several decades, my fascination with her books slowly faded.

However, when I recently visited Wharton's The Mount in the Berkshires, my passion for her writing rekindled. There's something awe-inspiring about visiting the locations where some of my favorite authors actually penned the words I devoured in high school and college. Doing the research for this book was a dream come true.

My chance to walk in the footsteps of the authors featured in *Ghost Writers* was a true gift. I'm grateful for all of the people I met along the way, including John Zaffis, Tabitha King, J.W. Ocker, Christopher Rondina, Susan Wilson, Robert Oakes, Gare Allen, Richard Estep, Peter Muise, Jack Kenna, Thomas D'Agostino, and Joseph Citro. Special thanks to Joni Mayhan for penning the book's foreword and directing me to Shaman Michael Robishaw when I needed help.

Photographers Jason Baker and Frank C. Grace deserve a supernatural slap on the back for capturing the eerie aesthetic of the main haunts featured in this book. I would also like to thank Amy Lyons from Globe Pequot for her support during the process of putting *Ghost Writers* together.

Thanks to my mother, Deborah Hughes Dutcher, for being there when I need her most and my family and friends—including Andrew Warburton who traveled with me to many of the haunted locations featured in the book—for their continued support. My high-school journalism teacher, Beverly Reinschmidt, also deserves kudos for inspiring me to keep writing.

Ghost Writers is dedicated to my stepfather, Paul Dutcher. His adventurous spirit lives on.

Each chapter of *Ghost Writers* begins with a quote from a featured author. If I had to choose my favorite line pulled from the pages of the book that terrified me the most, it would be King's *The Shining*. "Monsters are real, and ghosts are real too," King wrote. "They live inside us, and sometimes, they win."

SOURCES

Updated excerpts from my first eleven books, including *Wicked Salem: Exploring Lingering Lore and Legends, 13 Most Haunted in Massachusetts,* and *Haunted Boston Harbor* were featured in *Ghost Writers: The Hallowed Haunts of Unforgettable Literary Icons.*

The material in this book is drawn from published sources, including my articles in *DigBoston* and issues of the *Berkshire Eagle, Boston Globe, Boston Herald, CTNow* from *The Hartford Courant, Daily Free Press, The New York Times, The Observer,* and North Andover's *Eagle-Tribune,* and television programs such as Travel Channel's *Ghost Adventures* and *A Haunting* and SyFy's *Ghost Hunters.* Several books on New England's paranormal history were used and cited throughout the text. Other New England–based websites and periodicals, such as Peter Muise's New England Folklore, Curbed, OTIS: Odd Things I've Seen, Where The Ghosts

Edith Wharton's library at The Mount in Lenox, Massachusetts. PHOTO COURTESY DEPOSIT PHOTOS.

Live, Q1065-FM's blog as well as the websites for the Harriet Beecher Stowe Center and National Park Service served as sources.

Many of the classics, such as Nathaniel Hawthorne's *The House of the Seven Gables,* Harriet Beecher Stowe's *Uncle Tom's Cabin,* and Edith Wharton's *The Age of Innocence*, are cited throughout *Ghost Writers* and the works by the authors are highly recommended as supplemental reading.

I also conducted first-hand interviews, and some of the material is drawn from my own research. My former history-based tours, Wicked Salem, hosted at Wicked Good Books, Boston Haunts, and my Harvard Square Ghost Tour were also major sources and generated original content. It should be noted that ghost stories are subjective, and I have made a concerted effort to stick to the historical facts, even if it resulted in debunking an alleged encounter with the paranormal.

Andrews, Joseph L. *Revolutionary Boston*, Lexington, and Concord. Beverly, MA: Commonwealth Editions, 2002.

Baltrusis, Sam. *Ghosts of Boston: Haunts of the Hub*. Charleston, SC: The History Press, 2012.

———. *Ghosts of Salem: Haunts of the Witch City*. Charleston, SC: The History Press, 2014.

———. *Haunted Boston Harbor*. Charleston, SC: The History Press, 2016.

———. *13 Most Haunted Crime Scenes Beyond Boston*. Boston, MA: Sam Baltrusis, 2016.

———. *Wicked Salem: Exploring Lingering Lore and Legends*. Guilford, CT: Globe Pequot Press, 2019.

Balzano, Christopher. *Haunted Objects: Stories of Ghosts on Your Shelf.* Iola, WI: Krause Publications, 2012.

Boyer, Paul, and Stephen Nissenbaum. *Salem Possessed: The Social Origins of Witchcraft*. Cambridge, MA: Harvard University Press, 1974.

Cahill, Robert Ellis. *Haunted Happenings.* Salem, MA: Old Saltbox Publishing House, Inc., 1992.

———. *New England's Ghostly Haunts*. Peabody, MA: Chandler-Smith Publishing House, Inc., 1983.

———. *New England's Witches and Wizards*. Peabody, MA: Chandler-Smith Publishing House, Inc., 1983.

D'Agostino, Thomas. *A Guide to Haunted New England*. Charleston, SC: The History Press, 2009.

Dudley, Dorothy. *Theatrum Majorum: The Cambridge of 1776*. Whitefish, MT: Kessinger Publishing, 2007.

Forest, Christopher. *North Shore Spirits of Massachusetts*. Atglen, PA: Schiffer Publishing, 2003.

Guiley, Rosemary Ellen. *Haunted Salem*. Mechanicsburg, PA: Stackpole Books, 2011.

Hall, Thomas. *Shipwrecks of Massachusetts Bay*. Charleston, SC: The History Press, 2012.

Hauk, Dennis William. *Haunted Places: The National Directory*. New York: Penguin Group, 1996.

Hill, Frances. *Hunting For Witches*. Carlisle, MA: Commonwealth Editions, 2002.

Jasper, Mark. *Haunted Inns of New England*. Yarmouthport, MA: On Cape Publications, 2000.

Kampas, Barbara Pero. *The Great Fire of 1914*. Charleston, SC: The History Press, 2008.

Macken, Lynda Lee. *Haunted Salem & Beyond*. Forked River, NJ: Black Cat Press, 2001.

Mayhan, Joni. *Dark and Scary Things*. Gardner, MA: Joni Mayhan, 2015.

Muise, Peter. *Legends and Lore of the North Shore*. Charleston, SC: The History Press, 2014.

Nadler, Holly Mascott. *Ghosts of Boston Town: Three Centuries of True Hauntings*. Camden, ME: Down East Books, 2002.

Ocker, J.W. *Poe-Land: The Hallowed Haunts of Edgar Allan Poe*. Woodstock, VT: The Countryman Press, 2014.

Ogden, Tom. *Haunted Greenwich Village*. Guilford, CT: Globe Pequot Press, 2012.

Powers, Edwin. *Crime and Punishment in Early Massachusetts*. Boston, MA: Beacon Press, 1966.

Rapaport, Diane. *The Naked Quaker: True Crimes and Controversies*. Beverly, MA: Commonwealth Editions, 2007.

Revai, Cheri. *Haunted Massachusetts: Ghosts and Strange Phenomena of the Bay State*. Mechanicsburg, PA: Stackpole Books, 2005.

Roach, Marilynne. *The Salem Witch Trials: A Day-by-day Chronicle of a Community Under Siege*. Lanham, MD: Taylor Trade Publishing, 2002.

Rule, Leslie. *When the Ghost Screams: True Stories of Victims Who Haunt*. Kansas City, MO: Andrews McMeel Publishing, 2006.

Tucker, Elizabeth. *Haunted Halls: Ghostlore of American College Campuses*. Jackson: University Press of Mississippi, 2007.

Wilson, Susan. *Literary Trail of Greater Boston*. Boston, MA: Houghton Mifflin Company, 2000.

―――. *Boston Sites and Insights*. Boston, MA: Beacon Press, 2004.

Wilhelm, Robert. *Murder & Mayhem in Essex County*. Charleston, SC: The History Press, 2011.

Zwicker, Roxie J. *Haunted Pubs of New England: Raising Spirits of the Past*. Charleston, SC: The History Press, 2007.

INDEX

ABOUT THE AUTHOR

Sam Baltrusis, author of *Wicked Salem: Exploring Lingering Lore and Legends*, has penned eleven historical-based ghost books, including *Ghost Writers*. He has been featured on several national television shows, including Destination America's *Haunted Towns*, the Travel Channel's *Haunted USA* on Salem, and served as Boston's paranormal expert on the Biography Channel's *Haunted Encounters*. In 2019 he was featured on the 100th episode of *A Haunting* that aired on the Travel Channel. Baltrusis is a sought-after lecturer who speaks at dozens of paranormal-related events scattered throughout New England, including an author discussion at the Massachusetts State House and paranormal conventions he produced called the Plymouth ParaCon in 2018 and the Berkshire's MASS Para-Con in 2019. In the past, he has worked for VH1, MTV.com, *Newsweek*, and ABC Radio as well as a regional stringer for the *New York Times*. Visit SamBaltrusis.com for more information.

Doppelgänger? Author Sam Baltrusis specializes in historical haunts and has been featured on several national television shows sharing his experiences with the paranormal. *Photo by Frank C. Grace.*